BOOKS
BY
GEORGE PLIMPTON

THE RABBIT'S UMBRELLA (FOR CHILDREN)

OUT OF MY LEAGUE

WRITERS AT WORK, VOLUMES I-VIII (ED.)

PAPER LION

THE BOGEY MAN

THE AMERICAN LITERARY ANTHOLOGY, VOLUMES I-III (ED.)

AMERICAN JOURNEY: THE TIMES OF ROBERT F. KENNEDY (WITH JEAN STEIN)

PIERRE'S BOOK (ED.)

MAD DUCKS AND BEARS

ONE FOR THE RECORD

ONE MORE JULY

SHADOW BOX

SPORTS (WITH NEIL LEIFFER)

A SPORTS BESTIARY (WITH ARNOLD ROTH)

EDIE: AN AMERICAN BIOGRAPHY (WITH JEAN STEIN)

D.V. (WITH CHRISTOPHER HEMPHILL)

FIREWORKS: A HISTORY AND CELEBRATION

OPEN NET

THE CURIOUS CASE OF SIDD FINCH

THE WRITER'S CHAPBOOK (ED.)

THE PARIS REVIEW ANTHOLOGY (ED.)

THE LARGER AGENDA SERIES

THE X FACTOR

GEORGE PLIMPTON

WHITTLE DIRECT BOOKS

Photographs: Horseshoe match, Enrico Ferorelli, page 2; Gene Scott, Bermuda News Bureau/*Tennis Week* library, page 11; Bill Curry, Joey Ivansco/Stock South ©1990, page 13; Willie Davis, AP/Wide World, page 22; Anthony O'Reilly, inset photo, Alan D. Levenson, rugby photo provided by H.J. Heinz Company, page 23; Thomas J. Watson Jr., Mark Seliger/Onyx, page 26; Henry Kravis, Jonathan Levine/Onyx, page 40; Bob Beamon, Tony Duffy/Allsport USA, page 53; Peter Buterakos by Larry Fink, page 57; Michael Novak, Diana Walker/Gamma Liaison, page 63.

Library of Congress Catalog Card Number: 90-70577
Plimpton, George
The X Factor
ISBN 0-9624745-4-1
ISSN 1046-364X

The Larger Agenda Series

The Larger Agenda Series presents original short books by distinguished authors on subjects of importance to managers and policymakers in business and the public sector.

The series is edited and published by Whittle Communications L.P., an independent publishing company. A new book appears approximately every other month. The series reflects a broad spectrum of responsible opinions. In each book the opinions expressed are those of the author, not the publisher or the advertiser.

I welcome your comments on this unique endeavor.

William S. Rukeyser
Editor in Chief

CONTENTS

HORSESHOES
WITH THE
PRESIDENT

George Bush was just a week or so away from becoming the president of the United States. I was in Washington on assignment for *Sports Illustrated* to interview him about his athletic career.

We talked in the living room of the vice-president's official residence at the Naval Observatory. Mrs. Bush was with us, working on a needlepoint design of flowers. The atmosphere was very relaxed. The interview went well. Mr. Bush talked a lot about fishing—how it gave him time to relax from the rigors of work and to do some contemplative thinking. He quoted Izaak Walton's line about how the days a man spends fishing ought not to be deducted from his time on earth. He'd had only one long spell of government duty without fishing, and that was when he served as chief of the U.S. Liaison Office in Peking. Even there he'd had a chance. At a Soviet Embassy party he was invited to sit in a boat at one end of a ceremonial pool, while at the other an army of beaters got into the water and started driving a school of large carp toward him.

"Scary," Mr. Bush said. "Hundreds of these gigantic carp crashing around in the water. We waited for them with nets on the end of poles."

Barbara Bush remembered that what was caught was immediately cleaned by the Russian kitchen staff and prepared to take home. "The Russians had a beautiful complex built during the time of Peter the Great," she said. "They entertained a lot."

"Hockey games," the president-elect said. "On the lake. I was never much of a skater, so I didn't go out on the ice. I don't like to do things I can't do well. I don't dance well, so I don't dance.

"See this scar here?" he asked suddenly. He pointed to the back of his hand. A six-pound bluefish off Florida had nipped him. "Then I've got a scar here close to my eyebrow from a collision trying to head a ball playing soccer at Andover. Can't see it? Well, how about *this* one?" He pulled his shirt away from his neck to reveal a prominent bump on his right shoulder blade. "Got that one playing mixed doubles with Barbara at Kennebunkport. Ran into a porch."

"His mother always said that it was my shot," Barbara Bush said. "I didn't run for it, so he did. She was probably right."

The president-elect smiled and shrugged his shoulders. "Popped the shoulder out," he said. "Separated."

"After that, they moved the porch," his wife said with a smile.

Bush said that he had been playing tennis since he was about 5. He had stopped playing singles not long after grade school and concentrated on doubles, largely because his ground strokes were "terrible," except for a backhand chip return of service that drops at the feet of the oncoming server and that he referred to as "the falling leaf."

A number of other home-grown phrases have developed in the Bush family over the years, and I was told what some of them were. A weak shot elicits the disdainful cry "power outage!" The most esoteric is "unleash Chiang!"—from the hue and cry in government circles

The author startled the president-elect by throwing his shoes so that they revolved parallel to the ground—a style used by most topflight pitchers.

in reference to his recovery from political adversity there during the primaries. We watched the red horseshoe leave his hand, turn over once in flight, drop toward the pit with its prongs forward, and, with a dreadful clang, collect itself around the stake. A ringer! A total of 16 points and victory for the president-elect. He flung his arms straight up in triumph, a tremendous smile on his face. From her chair Jenna began yelping pleasantly.

I said as follows: "Nerts!"

I couldn't recall the last time I had used that antique expression. The president-elect came toward me, his hand outstretched. "Isn't that great!" he said as I congratulated him. He wasn't talking about his win but the fact that the game had been so much fun. I agreed with him. "*Heaven!*" he said.

We walked back to the residence. Up on the porch, Barbara Bush suggested that we leave our shoes, muddy from the horseshoe pitch, by the front door, so we wouldn't track mud on the carpets. I stepped out of my loafers. One of my socks had a hole in it. My big toe shone briefly until I pulled the sock forward. It dangled off the front of my foot and flopped as I followed the president-elect into the house. He wanted to give me a tour of the premises. I followed him upstairs, first to his closet-sized office with its photographs of the Cigarette boat *Fidelity*, which he takes out for bluefishing, and a mounted bonefish (TEN POUNDS, EIGHT OUNCES reads the plaque under it) with a little rubber shark riding its back, tossed up there by a grandchild.

We then went up to a dormitory-like room at the top of the house, where the older Bush children bunk out on the floor in sleeping bags when they come to visit. The nearest thing to a trophy case is up there—a shelf cluttered with the kind of shoe-box mementos one might find in the back of a teenager's closet: scuffed baseballs—one of them, I noted, signed by Joe DiMaggio with the inscription, "You make the office look great"; a football autographed by Roger Staubach, who wrote "Thanks for giving a darn about friends"; a Keith Hernandez model first-baseman's mitt; a Chicago Cubs pennant; a 1988 Dodgers World Series baseball cap; an NASL soccer ball; two construction worker's hard hats; and a blood-red Arkansas Razorback novelty hat shaped like a boar's head. The president-elect took the hat off the shelf and tried it on, the snout poking over his forehead.

"I'm not sure it suits you, sir," I said. "It would startle your constituency."

"Not in Arkansas," he said, putting it back.

He picked up one of the baseballs and began tossing it in his hand. "Nowadays the only time I handle these is throwing out ceremonial balls." He began describing an embarrassing moment when, hampered by a bulletproof vest, he had bounced a ball halfway to the Houston Astros catcher. "You tend to forget the distance," he said. "It's a question of raising your sights. You learn. Next time it's going to be right on target."

As we came down the stairs, a small group was standing in the foyer. I recognized members of the White House staff: Dan Quayle, the vice-president-elect; John Sununu, the chief of staff; Nick Brady, the secretary of the Treasury; and Brent Scowcroft, the national security adviser. Apparently the president-elect had scheduled a staff meeting. The toe of my stocking hung over a step. Sununu seemed to know something about my career as a participatory journalist. "Hey," he called up merrily. "A new Cabinet member?"

The president-elect went to the door with me. As I stepped back into my loafers he urged me to come back for a rematch. He said that as soon as possible a horseshoe court was going to be installed at the White House. "When the horseshoe court is ready, there'll be a ribbon-cutting ceremony. Got to come down for that."

I said I would. "But I'm bringing my own cowboy hat next time."

On the plane trip back to New York, I considered the Duke of Wellington's remark that the only thing to compare with the melancholy of a battle lost was that of a battle won. I wasn't so sure—at least not in my case. The president-elect was probably at this very moment leaning forward out of his chair at the Naval Observatory, chortling with delight and telling Quayle, Sununu, Scowcroft, Brady, and the rest of them what fun it had been—that he'd really cleaned that fellow's clock.

I began murmuring to myself. What had gone wrong? Probably I had let sympathy creep into my mind. I wasn't mentally prepared to apply the finishing measure—the killer instinct was missing, what I had heard called the X Factor, the ingredient that produced winners. Certainly *he* had it: witness that last extraordinary shot ("remember Iowa!"); witness that even such an insignificant act as throwing a ceremonial ball to a catcher had been evaluated: the next time he would raise his sights so that it would be right on target.

I began to feel sorry for myself. Shabby coat. I could feel the leather of my shoe with my toe. Things hadn't been going well elsewhere. The literary magazine, *The Paris Review*, which I have headed since its founding in the early '50s, had lost money yet again—for the 35th straight year. Was there a connection—losing here, losing there?

What was needed, I decided, was a revamping, a reevaluation. The symbolic nexus was the horseshoe match. The president-elect had asked me to come to Washington to play him again. Perhaps, in the interim, a change in attitude could be effected, a leaf turned, a new being constituted—competitive, confident, practical: a winner! I ordered a drink.

One course of action, naturally, would be to persuade my fellow tenants in New York City to let me set up a horseshoe court on the roof or in the cellar somewhere, so that I could practice day after day and perhaps even bring in a horseshoe expert for some coaching, who after a week or so would proclaim, "Hey, hey, now we're getting somewhere." But somehow that did not seem quite in the spirit of things: the president, occupied with the national debt by then, world crises here and there, and presumably (though one could never tell) unable to get down to the Rose Garden or wherever the horseshoe pitch was going to be built, would not be able to keep his hand in.

Much more appropriate would be to prepare myself psychologically. I would ask advice of sports psychologists, Zen masters, motivators, gurus, people who had been enormously successful in other fields, corporate CEOs, general managers, coaches, topflight athletes, and, pumped up with what they had been able to offer, I would arrive in Washington (with a new pair of socks) and try again.

The plane turned and I could see the lights of New York. I felt more cheerful. The humiliation had begun to slip away. The man next to me had pulled a fedora over his eyes to keep the light out and had fallen asleep. He would want to hear that I had been playing horseshoes with the president-elect. I cleared my throat loudly.

"What a beautiful night for flying."

Louis Turner
Pilot, Seattle

Our planes are equipped with Category III-A avionics, the most advanced in the industry. Which means that our pilots can land in weather when others can't. But more importantly, that we can deliver your shipments on time. When others might be late.

THE QUEST BEGINS

CHAPTER 2

A few days later, I telephoned Gene Scott, one of the great athletes Yale University has produced—a nine-letter man (in soccer, hockey, and tennis), a member of the Davis Cup team, and the successful editor-publisher of *Tennis Week*. Perhaps he would have some ideas about preparing for the rematch. He knew Bush. We could chat about the X Factor.

Billy Talbert, the tennis star, was the first person I ever heard use that term. In Paris, in the 1950s, somebody had asked him what constituted winning a championship. He replied that an X Factor was involved. Pressed on what that meant, he said he was using the word to describe a quality beyond natural gifts. In a close match, the outcome is determined by only 3 or 4 points, and the winner of those points, Talbert said, is usually endowed with this mysterious component. Added to the player's natural ability, it provides a kind of boost, like an afterburner kicking in. Talbert himself was the embodiment of the X Factor—slight, not especially fast, certainly not overpowering, and yet through savvy, spirit, and determination he had run up an astonishing record. He had won three national championships and, with different partners (usually Gardnar Mulloy or Tony Trabert), had won 35 championships in doubles.

When I reached Scott I said, "Guess what. I've just run into an X Factor."

After a pause he asked, "What are you talking about?"

I described how I'd gone down to Washington and in the course of things had played horseshoes in a match with George Bush.

"He beat you."

"Yes."

"I'm not surprised."

"He had the X Factor."

"Of course."

"Well, it was close," I said. I asked him how I would have done if we'd played tennis.

"He'd have beaten you. Technically, you have a better game, but you don't have much confidence in it. Bush, on the other hand, has an opinion of his game that far exceeds his ability: he simply has the confidence and the belief that he will prevail."

He started in on an interesting list of tennis players who, like Bush, had a kind of psychic energy that made them better than the sum of their parts. "Bitsy Grant—'The Giant-Killer,' they called him; Bobby Riggs; of course, Ted Schroeder. Schroeder was a player who was helpless in the backcourt, didn't like to play there, so he was forever charging the net on his own serve or chipping and charging on receipt of service—all of this especially effective on grass, on which all the major events in those days were played."

"What about the modern era?" I asked.

"Michael Chang," Scott said after a pause. "He has no visible overpowering strengths. No volley. No backhand. No offensive attitudes. But he runs well. A good athlete with a great quantity of moxie. He looks across the net and wants nothing more than to cut these big guys down to size." He snapped his fingers. "Jimmy Connors, of course. Great example. Mechanically, the guy's not much. But from the very beginning he was pumped full of confidence by his mother and Bill Reardon."

Somewhat tentatively, I asked Scott if there was any quick road to achieving this giant-killer characteristic, this X Factor, this attitude.

He laughed and said that one possibility was to diminish my height. "Get small," he said. "One thing about being small is that you get sick and tired of losing, and you figuratively become tall as a consequence. Of course," he said, "it's better if you're born with that X Factor you were speaking of." From the rueful way he mentioned it, I could tell he felt that getting small was my only solution.

Tennis Week **editor-publisher Gene Scott's advice about finding the X Factor turned out to be rather ethereal.**

Scott was right about my tennis. I once described it as follows: I think I'm really quite a decent tennis player despite a perceptible hitch in the backhand stroke that causes the ball to float alarmingly, a serve that rests right on the edge of hysteria, a dismaying tactical sense that calls for the grandstand rather than the percentage shot (a drop shot executed from the baseline is one of my favorites), a running style that has something of the giraffe in it, and, above all, a morbid preoccupation during play with impending doom. Still, when the local yacht club tennis tournament rolls around in the last weeks of June, I enter it with an optimist's conviction that the opposition will be doing well to take a set from me as I move through the draw to the Fourth of July finals. The club has 197 members. The men's singles trophy, a Revere silver bowl, sits on the clubroom table. It is the smallest model Tiffany's offers, and one would be hard-pressed to load it up with more than seven or eight cashew nuts. I stare at it longingly. The runner-up trophy stands alongside. It is a fluted vase appropriate for a single long-stemmed rose, too thin for a name as lengthy as mine to be engraved on it without running back into itself. It shines its pristine polished light, however, and I persuade myself to find it acceptable if, by some chance . . .

My opponent in the first round is a tall, melancholy man who comes down to the courts carrying two aluminum rackets in their covers. During the warm-up his strokes are classic. Years of lessons and practice. I think of him as a mirror of myself. I had begun when I was 8—all those years on my grandparents' court with the apple basket of old tennis balls, trying to hit the handkerchief spread in the center of the service court. ("He aces Budge!" my inner voice exclaimed.) My grandmother had a parrot that flew around the place untrammeled. Its favorite perch was the wire backstop, where it teetered in the soft winds, its tail hanging down behind. It enjoyed the tennis and the only phrase it uttered, which it did constantly, was "love-40!"

My opponent begins to practice his serve. His mouth goes ajar as he hits it. He had played on the team at Amherst, I had heard. Very shy man. Low voice. Asks if I am ready. The match begins. He wins the toss and double-faults. He double-faults again. He begins to disintegrate. My serve. His first return of service hits the net in the adjacent court. "Bend your knees, you fat faggot!" he cries at himself. His rage mounts. "Oh suffering Jesus!" he cries. We play appalling tennis and I extinguish him. We meet at the net. "I played well today," I say. I have read somewhere that Rod Laver uses that phrase when he walks up to the net to comfort his defeated opponents. The Amherst man detests me. "Your game was a little off. I'd hate to run into it when it's on," I say. He grunts. A very pretty girl who has been watching turns out to be his wife. She comes out on the court and touches his hand. She has olive eyes and high cheekbones. She loathes me. They get into a very expensive car. They are going to a grand lunch somewhere. I stare after them.

Second round: the day is muggy. My opponent is a sandy-haired older man who wears a hearing aid. He is one of the club's best yachtsmen. He came in third in the Bermuda Race one year. He wears blue yachting sneakers and khaki shorts. His tennis style is awkward. He pushes at the ball. During the warm-up I do not make an error. The match begins. After 10 minutes he is ahead 3-0. He is steady. Everything comes back. I tighten up. I begin to play his game, patting the ball back. Rage begins to mount in me, first at him ("Why can't he hit the ball and play tennis like a man?") and then finally at myself. I berate myself, both verbally and physically. I cry out my name. I lift my racket and belt myself in the calf. A welt rises and throbs. He wins the first set. Play begins in the second. I net an easy volley. I refer to myself as an ox. The match is over. Nearly weeping with frustration, I walk to the net. Is he going to say something? He is. "I was really on today," he says. He puts out his hand. I murmur my apologies for

University of Kentucky coach Bill Curry, who was at Alabama until 1990, has the X Factor nailed down to five "overachieving" characteristics.

13

having played so badly. "Can I buy you a ginger ale or something?" he asks.

"Not for me," I say. I have a terrible thirst.

I go to my car. I am perspiring heavily. I stick to the seats. I think about the X Factor. Why hadn't it turned up? Why was it out *yachting*, or whatever? I wonder if I'll be able to stand the country-club buffet that night—the guy with the tall chef's hat standing behind the roast beef platter, *he* will know. I turn the ignition key. The motor hums. I put the top down. The wind will feel nice on the skin. I begin to feel a bit better. They are having a picnic on the rocks by Seal Head. They'll have brought ice-cold lemonade down in thermos bottles.

The X Factor is of extraordinary, even morbid, interest to sports journalists like myself, general managers, coaches, athletes, and indeed the general public. What *is* the ingredient that makes one athlete considerably better than another, though both are of equivalent physical skill? Even more mysterious, what is it that makes an entire *team* better than others, when the general makeup of all is about the same? Some ingredient is involved, a potion that people in all walks of life—from coaches to corporate CEOs—would go to extravagant lengths to obtain if it came in a small earthenware jug corked at its mouth.

I got a sense of what the jug's contents might be through a series of conversations with Bill Curry, an All-Pro center in the '70s and a successful coach at Georgia Tech, Alabama, and now the University of Kentucky. I got to know him when I was doing a participatory-journalism stint with the Baltimore Colts. I liked a story Curry told me about Willie Davis, the great defensive end at Green Bay, where Curry played his rookie year before going to the Colts. Davis had come to him in the locker room to give him a kind of mental tip that he had used to motivate himself ever since a game against the Eagles in 1960. As he left the field that day, the game over, Davis turned around and saw the stands emptying, and he realized that he was leaving something on the field—namely, regrets that he had not given the extra effort, the extra push . . . and that he was going to have to live with that regret for the rest of his life because there was no way that he could recapture that moment. He made up his mind then that he would never again look back at a football field or even a day's effort at what he was doing with any sense of regret. Curry told me that when watching Packer game films when the outcome was long decided, he always marveled at Davis's white-heat intensity throughout, never dogging it or taking it easy.

"What about the X Factor with teams?" I asked.

"Let me tell you," said Curry. "It all begins with the players having the capacity to focus. Without that, it just never happens. When I was a child I was fascinated by these little magnifying glasses—I'd get them out of Cracker Jack boxes. I could sit in the woods on a day when it was 35 degrees, and with the sun 93 million miles away I could be involved in a process that brought the rays that distance and centered them with a magnifying glass on one spot until a pile of leaves would burst into flame. A focus of energy. Everybody who has this X Factor has the capacity to zero in so totally. If you've ever looked at a picture of Bjorn Borg hitting a ball, look at his eyes. Ted Williams picking up the actual stitches on the baseball.

"So what I teach our teams is that you've got to focus on the task. Then I go on to give them the five characteristics of every great overachieving person I've ever studied. We teach these almost every day . . . to the staff, the team, anybody who'll listen."

He raised a finger.

"Number one—it really doesn't matter if it's Helen Keller or Wilma Rudolph or Vince Lombardi—is a kind of singleness of purpose. You see it when that little squirt Michael Chang goes on the court to hit a tennis ball. There's such a singleness of purpose that everything else is blocked out—the crowd noise, the weather conditions, the fact that the other guy can hit BBs and you can't—it doesn't matter; you're going to beat him anyhow. That's the first characteristic. The second is unselfishness. The capacity to give when other people won't or can't. When your legs won't move another step, somehow you make a move. In a team effort, it's the capacity to create the win with absolutely no concern for who gets the credit. It's an attitude that is just as applicable to business. In college I was an industrial-management major at Georgia Tech, which has turned out an astonishing number of CEOs who are among *Fortune* magazine's top 500. The chairmen of the boards of Delta, American Express, Phillips Petroleum—all those guys went to Georgia Tech. These are the ingredients that I found in those people: the ability to convey a sense of family and caring and concern with all different kinds of personalities. It comes with the leader being willing to serve, being willing to make himself the least. He walks in at six o'clock in the morning and makes the janitor feel important; he does unselfish things."

I mentioned that greed and selfishness were increasingly associated with business.

"Greed is not in my quotient," Curry said, "unless you define greed in an altruistic way, meaning every action is in a sense selfish. If Mother Teresa gets a warm feeling from feeding a starving child in India, she is being rewarded. She's not interested in making a million dollars, but she gets her reward. But if greed is defined as the accumulation of wealth for its own sake, that's the opposite of what we're talking about. One guy with that kind of motive can destroy a whole team. The Boston Celtics come down the court and if Larry Bird wanted to shoot all the time, the Celtics wouldn't have won all those championships. Bird can't jump, he can't run; the guy is a country boy. But when he gets on the court, he becomes magic because he is unselfish."

"What's the third characteristic?" I asked.

"Toughness. A champion is tough. But I don't mean gritting your teeth, foaming at the mouth, and hitting people on the side of the head. I mean being honest in your effort when other people are not being honest. Sticking to the principles of fair play and ethical behavior and out-conditioning, out-thinking, out-working your opponent rather than finding ways to bend the rules. That is real toughness, at least in the NCAA today. The real tough guys are able to suck it up and follow the rules, even when they're getting pasted. The gutless ones, the ones who are not tough, are the ones who have to break the rules to win; they aren't winners at all—in fact, they've never won a single match. When you commit a dishonest act, you lose power. When you refuse to denigrate yourself, there is a great power, a great X Factor, that accrues to your benefit. Norman Vincent Peale called it the Plus Factor. Homer Rice, the athletic director at Georgia Tech, calls it the Inner Power Success Force.

"The fourth characteristic I've found is that all champions are smart. It has nothing to do with IQ, with education. I don't know quite how to say it except that it's street smart, country smart . . . they just know their business. Certain people, like John Unitas or Bart Starr, come out of the huddle on the football field and, if you had to play against them, you'd know you were going to be cut to ribbons. It's partly intuitive, but it's also part training. It's knowing your business.

"The fifth one's the most important. Champions never quit. Sometimes I get up in front of the team and I say, 'Did you ever get in a fistfight with a guy you thought you were going to beat up really easily and you knock him down, turn to walk away, and you realize he's gotten up, and you knock him down, and the son of a gun gets up again, and it starts to dawn on you that this is going to be a long day? Before long, you're not knocking him down anymore; he's knocking *you* down. You've gotten in a fight with the wrong guy. He's not gonna quit.' Then it becomes a battle of the wills—like the old-time boxing matches when you had to put your toe to the line and they went 139 rounds. That was the ultimate contest: who would quit first. I remember an interviewer asking John McEnroe about Connors one time: 'What is it about Jimmy Connors?' McEnroe thought about it, and he said, 'You can beat him a hundred times in a row and he'll never admit it.' Lombardi said, 'I've never lost a game.' We thought he was nuts. Then we realized he meant that the clock ran out on him. His attitude never changed. He said, 'Winning is not the most important thing; it is the only thing.' When he elaborated on that he'd go on to say, 'Winning is not the most important thing; the *will* to win is the most important.' The game clock may run out, but the will continues.

"So, in short, champions have the capacity to focus. They have a singleness of purpose; they are unselfish—able to give when others can't and when there's no apparent reward; they are tough—meaning tough endurance-wise but also meaning willing to follow the rules when the competition will not; they are smart; and they just never quit. I think it goes across the board: business, politics, sports, life."

I told Curry that I planned to play President Bush in a game of horseshoes. A win was rather important. Did he have any practical advice?

He thought for a while. "Well, if I were going to play with the president of the United States, I would lose," he said with a grin, " . . . out of respect and awe for the office."

"I already have," I said. "We have a rematch coming up."

"Oh. Well, it depends how badly you want to win," Curry said. "If it's a social event, then I'd relax and not think about it. I'd play and I'd have fun. If you're into the X Factor thing you've been talking about, I'd get the best videotape there is on horseshoe pitching, study it, drill yourself. I'd visualize beating the president—the horseshoes coming down on the stake, seeing the score the way you want it, shaking hands with him. It will happen because you saw it in your mind. I'd call in the great experts. We bring in Jan Stenerud to work with our kickers, Joe Namath and Bart Starr to rub shoulders with the quarterbacks . . . see if they can instill the X Factor."

"And is that possible?" I asked.

"Sometimes," he said. "Of course, that's the fascinating thing about the X Factor. Each person has his own . . . a potential; so in that sense it's indefinable. . . . "

"Every day, I help the world's most stylish women get dressed."

Jeffrey Spiegel
Worldwide Account Executive, New York City

PartsBank®, the Federal Express warehousing, inventory control, and distribution service, allows designers to bring their latest creations in from Europe, into the finest stores, in just days. Giving retailers priceless extra days to sell them.

RUGBY
AND
WILD DUCKS

CHAPTER 3

I ran into Willie Davis, the great Green Bay defensive end, whose good nature had earned him the nickname Dr. Feelgood among his teammates. Since his football days he has become a CEO, sits on a number of important boards, and is considered as fine a businessman as he was a football player.

I asked Davis if his years at Green Bay had been of any value to him afterward. What about his coach, Vince Lombardi? I reminded him that when Jerry Kramer, his teammate, was asked if Lombardi had ulcers, he had replied, "No, but he is a carrier."

Davis laughed. "Lombardi," he said, still smiling. "I think the majority of us quickly identified the qualities we learned at Green Bay as being the keys to any success afterward. Lombardi often referred to the bridge between what we were doing for him and what came after. He would say to us, 'If you don't do it here, you're not going to turn it on in another life. If you can prove here what it takes to get it done, the next job is not going to be that different.'"

Davis went on to say that sports create a kind of arena in which you get a lot of quick answers—not only about yourself but about other people. Sports provide a kind of laboratory in which you can see how others perform under stress, playing out emotions, working toward a goal. "The basics in business," he said, "are really very similar."

I asked if Lombardi would have made a good CEO. Davis laughed and said that yes, he thought so. "He would always set a good example. Tough as he was on others, he was always prepared to do the same himself. You'd go by his office in Green Bay at midnight and you'd see his car parked outside the office. He was in there working. That was one of the impressions he left: Do as I do. Not just as I say."

"Willie," I asked, "do you remember a play in Philadelphia? Bill Curry described it to me once. . . ."

"Oh, yes," Davis said. "The moment of commitment. It was late in the third quarter. Billy Barnes made a great run around the other end. When the play started out I knew I could get over there to him and bring him down—I'd done it before—but then I began thinking, *why overextend myself?* There were other Packers over there. They could handle it. So I moved over there kind of casual, and there goes Barnes for 25, 30 yards. It was an important run because it was a third-down situation.

"Well, that play stuck in my mind. Indelible. If I'd gone at first opportunity, there's no doubt I would've reached Barnes and got him down. No doubt. Maybe we wouldn't have won the game, but I told myself that never again would I come out of a situation wondering if I could have done a job better. It's just as important to me today as it was then. Every day that's what I tell myself—not to let an opportunity slide by that I could have taken advantage of."

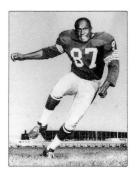

Willie Davis learned from his football days never to let an opportunity slide by—a lesson he's carried over to the business world.

I t was an interesting parallel to consider—sports and business. I brought it up in a conversation I had with Anthony O'Reilly, who is the head of H.J. Heinz Company. He was a great rugby player in the 1950s and '60s, star of Ireland, winner in his country of the equivalent of the Heisman Trophy. He loves the game of rugby with a great passion. Indeed, on one occasion he came out of retirement, long after he should have, but then vowed he would not do so again after his captain told him that his best effort against the opposing players had been to shake his jowls at them.

Outspoken, his voice a rich, rolling brogue one might associate with the Dublin Players theater group, he is a firm believer in the close correlation between sports and big business. In fact, three of the businesses he is involved in besides Heinz (a multinational newspaper company, an oil-and-gas exploration company, and an industrial holding group) have in their operations people who played rugby with him.

"They all exhibit very much the characteristics in their daily business lives that they did on the rugby field," he told me. "Those who were terriers on the rugby field turned out to be terriers in business. If you determine what business is all about and what the characteristics are that bring people to the top of the business pile, I think you'll find that a great parallel exists, especially in the competitive team sports. I don't find such parallels in the individual sports. Indeed, many of the characteristics in those—à la John McEnroe—would probably suggest a disqualification."

"You don't imagine McEnroe as a CEO?"

"I see him, perhaps, as the CEO of his own company," O'Reilly said with a grin, "in which he is the only member of the board, arguing with himself."

Thinking of McEnroe, I couldn't resist asking O'Reilly about what seems the most undisciplined and unruly aspect of rugby—the scrum, that oddest of the sporting conformations, insectlike, the legs churning under a carapace of human backs.

"What's it like in there?" I asked.

"It sounds like a men's locker room," O'Reilly said. "A lot of unfriendly advice is given from one side to the other. The basic conflict is a law of applied physics, because eight men scrum down against eight men. You'll remember the definition of the game of rugby—that while soccer is a gentleman's game played by thugs, rugby is a thug's game played by gentlemen. In rugby, just as in American football, there is a high level of controlled violence, which tests you against a lot of life's basic instinctive reactions. It requires a great deal of communality at the higher level; you quickly have the

Anthony O'Reilly, chairman of H.J. Heinz, perceives "a great parallel" between success in team sports and business. At left, O'Reilly the rugby star fends off a tackler in a 1958 match at Lands Downe Road in Dublin.

whole notion of collegiality . . . that is, a sense of a group of people having a common purpose. You learn the acme of team sports—the subjugation of individual ambition to the common purpose. The selection procedure has to be of the most rigorous kind, and the most ruthless: no nepotism, nobody's mommy or daddy or bank balance or what school one went to. It's a meritocracy out there on the rugby field, and that's the way a business should be run. If someone doesn't make it, you put him on the sidelines, or on the taxi squad, or get rid of him altogether."

O'Reilly railed against the star system that he felt was an unfortunate part not only of American team sports but also of business. "There has to be a certain sublimation in all of this," he said. "In order for a team to be invincible, there's got to be collective skills rather than individual brilliance. The teams I played on had no great stars. The New Zealanders, the best of the internationals, had stars, but they were of the muted variety. In business, the level of political drama within a company is exacerbated by an excess adulation of one or two people—the cult of the personality. America is particularly adept at taking a man and using him as an icon to explain business. Lee Iacocca is a classic example. Seven years ago he was voted the best CEO in the country. He got three quarters of the selection committee's votes. This year he got none. Now, does that mean he was better seven years ago than now? No. What happened seven years ago was that a trigger mechanism and voluntary quotas were put on the import of Japanese cars. So he was the beneficiary of protectionism. But now that's gone, his own costs have gone against him and . . . well, he looks like a real clown. I think that's an example of the wrong way to run a business. Heinz is not Tony O'Reilly, and Chrysler is not Lee Iacocca. What games like football teach us is that you must have basic qualifications and an ongoing rigorous education toward a common cause . . . properly motivated and massively compensated through the reward system."

I asked him about Vince Lombardi and his quote about winning being the only thing.

"I reject it," O'Reilly said. "I absolutely reject it. It's vulgar. It carries the seeds of destruction." He went on to say that his favorite quote was from Kipling's "If," which used to hang above the player's entrance to center court at Forest Hills: "If you can meet with Triumph and Disaster/And treat those two imposters just the same/ . . . you'll be a Man, my son!"

"The amateur sports that I played," O'Reilly said, "had that great Corinthian quality: we were playing for sport, and at the same time we were qualifying to be lawyers, doctors, dentists, and in the case of the Welsh, in that great democracy of players, bulldozer drivers, steel workers, tin puddlers. One chap who was a bulldozer driver said to me one day, 'The trouble with you university chaps is that you use great long words like *corrugated* and *marmalade*'—the only two long words he could come up with. But if I were in Wales looking for someone to do something that required integrity, the first person I'd call would be Corrugated Marmalade himself, because I know I'd be getting 100 percent of what he had to offer."

"But you wouldn't ask him to be a CEO?"

"No. Well, I wouldn't put him into a debate with Mr. Kissinger."

He told a story about Pete Dawkins that he felt illustrated the difference between the Corinthian attitudes of amateurism and the near-professionalism of collegiate sports in the United States. Dawkins had turned up at Oxford on a Rhodes scholarship, preceded, of course, by an extraordinary reputation as an athlete—a great career at West Point as a running back, which had won him the Heisman Trophy. At Oxford he played rugby, though his position on the team for the traditional Oxford-Cambridge match at Twickenham was by no means assured. At both Oxford and Cambridge only the 15 players picked to play in that game get their "blue," which is the equivalent of getting a letter at an American college. To receive a blue (the color for both universities is blue—Oxford dark and Cambridge light) means much more in the British scheme of things than earning a letter does in the U.S. "He played football for Michigan," say, has a fine ring, but it doesn't compare to what it means in England to say, "He has his blue—rugby, y'know."

The team captain decides who is to play and thus receive this high honor. At Oxford, the selection for the Oxford team takes place at a black-tie dinner at Balliol College during the week before the Tuesday on which the game is played every year.

"It was the contrast," O'Reilly said. "Here was Dawkins, who had gone through all the hoopla of the Heisman Trophy—radio, television, the huge press—standing rather nervously in his tuxedo, waiting to hear from the captain upstairs if he was going to be picked to play at Twickenham. It was not at all clear that he was good enough to get his blue.

"Well, the captain appeared from upstairs, picked out a dry sherry for himself, came over, and with that infuriating way the British have of looking at you as though they hadn't seen you for 42 years, when in fact you've both been in the shower room a half-hour before, he said, 'Oh, Dawkins, *there* you are.' Then, referring to the Tuesday game, he said, 'Oh, by the way, Dawkins, are you *free* next Tuesday?' And that's how the Heisman Trophy winner learned he'd won his blue!"

Another huge company that disapproves of the star system so derided by Tony O'Reilly would surely be IBM. In fact, Thomas J. Watson Jr., when he was the CEO, felt that IBM's astonishing resiliency was due not to the skill of its administrators (which I would have guessed) but to the power of its fundamental company guidelines. These were enunciated by the first of the Watsons, T. J. Sr., who joined IBM when he was 40, in 1914—having been fired as the general manager of National Cash Register Company and brought in to run a loose alliance of three small companies. These tenets can be put rather simply: to do every

Thomas J. Watson Jr., a retired chief executive of IBM, tried to preserve his father's policy of instilling family values in the company without stifling what they called the "wild ducks."

job well, to treat all people with dignity and respect, to appear neatly dressed, to be clear and forthright, to be eternally optimistic, and above all to be loyal. The various disciplines that evolved to sustain these family values are well known—a dress code (white shirts), no booze at company functions, among others.

At the same time, the Watsons always worried about the stifling effect such codes and disciplines might have on an organization: they were very much in favor of what they called wild ducks—*mavericks* would be the contemporary term. Wild ducks was a description based on a Søren Kierkegaard story about a farmer who put out so much feed for the wild ducks that after four or five years they didn't bother migrating; they grew so fat and lazy that they found it difficult to fly at all—the point being that you can tame a wild duck, but you can't teach him to be wild again.

Whatever the Watsons felt about wild ducks, conformity has certainly left its mark on IBM. Some years ago at the Fontainbleau Hotel in Miami Beach, I was to give speeches to a succession of IBM salesmen—600 at a time—who were members of what was called the Gold Circle. For selling a certain amount of IBM equipment, the membership was rewarded by a vacation in Miami and various entertainments, of which listening to me was supposed to be one. In their dark suits, the sensible ties over the white shirts, the salesmen trooped into the convention theater of the hotel, a plush emporium with seats that had been equipped with push-buttons so the audience could respond yes or no to questions asked of them, the tabulation flashing up on a huge screen behind the lectern on the stage. The IBM executives in charge of the meetings urged me to ask questions so that the buttons could be used—apparently it seemed appropriate that a vast company largely involved in a high-technology industry should avail itself of such an opportunity, however primitive!

The first day (I was scheduled to speak to four audiences) I forgot to ask any questions, but I do remember a backstage conversation immediately after I'd come off the stage. The IBM executives wanted me to remove something from my presentation. It was a mild story about a friend of mine who had been trapped in a Port-O-Let during a golf tournament while Arnold Palmer, just outside the door, was trying to concentrate on hitting a shot. It was a funny story; at worst the only off-color part of it was the mention of the Port-O-Let, which I suppose, in the minds of the executives, put the story in the outhouse category. The IBM people were quite apologetic about their primness, but they were also firm. The year before, O. J. Simpson had stunned them (though not necessarily the audience) with some off-color material. It had come unexpectedly as they stood offstage, looking in from the wings at the great athlete standing at midstage telling bawdy jokes, and they were unable to do anything about it.

I was somewhat startled at their reaction to my story and especially that *I* was being criticized. I don't know any dirty jokes or stories. My recriminatory arsenal usually comprises such epithets as "drat," "dad-blame," "Lordy," and "for Pete's sake." To be warned about off-color material and to have a story deleted from my presentation . . . well, it was almost heady! In any case, I agreed to remove the Port-O-Let story.

Once again I was urged to ask questions of the audience so the push-button system could be used. The next afternoon I found a place in midspeech to do so. I told my audience that James Thurber, the *New Yorker* humorist, had once suggested that 95 percent of the males in America put themselves to sleep striking out the batting order of the New York Yankees (much easier now than then, I said to raise a laugh) and that I had always wondered if this figure was accurate. Perhaps they could help me. I asked how many agreed with Mr. Thurber. The members of the audience murmured as they bent over their armrests.

I have forgotten the exact figure that flashed up on the screen behind me, except that it was a number well below the Thurber estimate.

I then gave them an alternate. How many of them put themselves to sleep at night dreaming of Bo Derek, the willowy actress whose presence in a film called *10* (in which she appeared in a white bathing suit and less) had made a considerable impact on the public? Once again, the murmur of voices, shadowy fingers probing in the semidark for the buttons in the armrests.

When the tabulations were done, the figure suddenly flashed on the screen—69! Filling the back of the stage, the number glowed there, immutable, stunning us. A titter rose. It was evident that my audience knew the number's sexual connotation. Suddenly someone couldn't contain himself and burst into a violent guffaw. It ignited the rest—600 people, finally, pounding their knees, rocking back and forth, letting loose with such a concussion of laughter that I felt it was almost palpable, swaying as I stood on the stage in its gusts sweeping across the footlights . . . of such magnitude that it was as if all those years of putting on the white shirts and sensible ties and the blue suits and the rest was preparing one for this ironic, mighty smack at the whole system. It was as if Watson Sr. himself had appeared in his blue suit, etc., and congratulated them for being elected to the Gold Circle, and stated how proud IBM was of their contribution, and then, being a wild duck, had turned and mooned them from center stage.

Finally the laughter died away. Shaken, I thanked the audience for its cooperation (which got them laughing again), and I went on with the talk. From time to time, irrespective of what I was saying, a pocket of laughter would start up again and die away, like the mutter of a summer storm.

In the wings after it was over, I said I was sorry. "It was really out of my control."

They understood. Of *course* they understood. They were the ones who had urged me to use the system. The executive group kept what I thought was a pretty stiff upper lip about what had happened. They didn't seem very much amused. Perhaps they were annoyed that the audience had started laughing. They seemed like teachers whose kindergarten pupils had suddenly erupted out of control.

But the next afternoon they seemed much more cheerful. "You can use the buttons," they said. "Everything's been fixed."

"What?"

"You can ask them about Bo Derek."

"I can?"

"What we've done is to program that number *right out of the system!*"

"I'm here to answer your questions around the clocks."

Mary Lucus-Fisher
Senior Customer Service Agent, Sacramento

Whatever you need to know—from prices, packaging tips and customs regulations
to the status of your shipment, pick-up to delivery—our Customer Service Centers can tell
you, quickly and courteously. Twenty-four hours a day.

RAGE AND MOTIVATION

The president telephoned. It was about a month after his inauguration. At the time of the call I was sitting in the office of *The Paris Review* in New York. It is cramped. A bicycle hangs from hooks in the ceiling; the editors have to duck under it to sit at their desks. Sometimes six editors are crammed in under there. One of them picked up the phone and, with a startled look on his face, handed it to me. "It's the White House calling," he said. "The president." He handed me the receiver.

"Yes, Mr. President," I said.

It wasn't the president, of course, but a secretary down the line. After a while the president himself came on—his voice unmistakable and so clear that my fellow editors, leaning out of their chairs, could listen in.

"Nice to hear from you, sir," I said cheerfully.

He had called to invite me to Washington to be on hand when the horseshoe pitch was inaugurated at a ribbon-cutting ceremony. Some horseshoe experts were coming in, and we'd get a chance to play again. The rematch.

I looked in my calendar and discovered I was scheduled to be in San Diego on that day.

"I can't do it, sir."

"What?"

"I've been asked to be the grand marshal of a crew regatta," I said miserably.

"Get it over with and catch the red-eye back East," the president suggested. "Rest up here at the White House. We have lots of room," he explained, as if asking a guest to a country home.

My editors nodded their heads.

I explained that my presence was required throughout the regatta, that I was expected to hand out trophies at the final ceremonies. "Yale has sent some shells," I said feebly. "They may win. . . . "

The president finally gave up trying to convince me. "Well, we'll have to postpone the rematch," he said. "We'll miss you at the ceremonies." He said he looked forward to the match when it could be arranged, and hung up.

My staff stared at me.

I shrugged my shoulders. "It gives me more time to prepare."

At dinner that night, word got around the table that the president had called.

"He's trying to get you to run the country for a day," someone gibed.

The guests looked down the length of the table. I told them that years ago President Kennedy, whom I knew and who was interested in my participatory-journalism stints, had done exactly that—invited me down to run the country for a day. "Then he picked the day," I said. "February 31st!"

"And what day has Bush picked?"

"Not germane," I answered. "He only wants me to play horseshoes." I mentioned—not all that facetiously—that I thought beating him would be a turning point in my career, that my endeavors from that time on would have an entirely new . . . well, the word I used was *heft*.

"Heft?"

To talk about one's state of mind is difficult enough, so I dropped it. But the talk about preparing for the horseshoe match continued around the table. The suggestion I remember best came from someone who must have been a history major at college: "I've always heard that every great athlete was motivated by a kind of controlled rage. It's not only sports. The energy of all sorts of successful people is fueled by an anger—sometimes conscious, often not. It galvanizes. It is directed against any number of targets—authority, family, race, indignity, another's principles—and one is driven to success out of *spite*.

"Now, I understand you're a Democrat," he said, looking up from the other end of the table. "What you need to do is think up every indignity the Republicans have ever heaped on society over the years—in no particular order, the Depression, McCarthyism, Watergate, James Watt, Crédit Mobilier, Teapot Dome, robber barons, Smoot-Hawley, anti-unionism, the '87 crash . . . you let all this simmer, and then take it down to Washington and mentally level it at Bush. Controlled rage, that's what it is. Think Teapot Dome!"

"Very funny," my dinner companion said afterward in the taxi.

"But not very helpful."

"You're much too serious about all this," she said. "Incidentally, what did you mean by that word, 'heft'?"

"I have no idea," I said. "It just popped out."

The guest at dinner was certainly on to something—controlled rage was very likely a part of the X Factor. Bill Russell, the Boston Celtics star center, once told me that he would lie in his hotel room before a game and imagine that he was the sheriff in a western cow town where a gang of black hats (the Philadelphia 76ers or the Atlanta Hawks, whatever team the Celtics were playing that night) had turned up and were running roughshod through the place, beating up people and gunning down a few. He would work up a coldblooded rage and stalk them through the dusty streets, knocking them off one by one. Athletes learn to turn on this controlled rage—some quicker than others. Bill Curry told me that before the Colts went out onto the field, Mike Curtis, the middle linebacker they called "Animal," would ask a teammate to belt him alongside the helmet, *wallop* him, which would ignite the rage, like a light switch clicked on.

Over the years I've been just as interested in *uncontrolled* rage as in controlled, perhaps more so because it's much more interesting to write about. I have always treasured the sight of Tommy Heinsohn, when he coached the Boston Celtics, leveling a kick at the bucket that contained oranges to suck on, missing it, and having his loafer, a very large model, sailing up into the mezzanine. In baseball, the water cooler was traditionally the target of rage, though other inanimate objects were often larger. Chicago pitcher Mad Monk Meyers was sitting peacefully enough in a bathroom stall one afternoon, when suddenly rage over some indignity on the pitcher's mound swept over him; he got up and ripped the latrine door off its hinges. Hank Greenberg once told me that his pitcher-teammate Fred Hutchinson used to break light bulbs, swatting at them with his glove as he headed down the corridor that led from the Detroit Tigers dugout back to the locker room. When he later became a manager, the fungo bat became the instrument of his frustration—he would pound it on the dugout steps until it snapped. Usually three or four fungo bats, which are used for fielding practice, will last a club through the season. But the Tigers would order up a dozen or so because they knew that Hutchinson would break most of them during the summer. Jim Brosnan, the ex-Cubs and Reds pitcher, who wrote a wonderful baseball book called *The Long Season*, told me this about Hutchinson: "When the

Tigers lost, he was no one to live with. His wife would hear the news on the radio or watch it on television, and she'd turn and warn the children. One time Hutch came home after a Tiger loss—sometimes he walked miles along Michigan Avenue—and to everyone's surprise he seemed to be making an effort to keep his temper in check. He sat down for dinner with his family. He didn't say much. Then, just as he was getting up from his dessert, he turned and threw a punch in frustration, and he busted a hole in the wall right behind his chair. His wife cried out, 'Look, Hutch, what you've done!' and he growled, 'Hang a picture over it,' and stomped out."

Hutchinson would have felt very much at home with an Indian tribe called the Yanomamö living in southern Venezuela and northern Brazil. Described in 1988 by a sociologist named Napoleon Chagnon, its members operate socially in a constant state of rage. Indeed, a quick, fiery temper and a readiness to use violence are considered virtues in their culture. Wives, as might be expected, have a miserable time. The males not only work themselves into a rage at the slightest provocation, but seek to bring others to the boiling point with insults, face slaps, and so forth, which Chagnon describes as being close to an imitation of the power-announcing behavior of apes.

One might think this a complete reversal of the decorum required of our Western culture, where anger (except in the case, as we've seen, of the odd athlete) is kept pretty much in check, certainly in the genteel circles of big business. Not so. I have been reading Bryan Burrough and John Helyar's *Barbarians at the Gate*, an account of the largest takeover in Wall Street history—the fight to control RJR Nabisco during October and November of 1988. As I turned the pages, it struck me how often the players in the drama behaved like members of the Yanomamö. What follows is by no means a complete listing:

Weigl stormed . . . and stormed . . . and stormed.

He [Horrigan] began to cry, his fury and frustration producing tears that streamed down his cheeks in torrents.

Johnson simmered.

Kohlberg exploded.

Cy Lewis hit the roof.

Spangler stewed.

Kravis began to grow angry. "I can't believe this," he fumed.

Beck was fuming.

Tempers flared.

Kravis could barely contain his anger.

After much gnashing of teeth, Kohlberg . . .

Cohen's anger quickly gave way to shock.

"Goddamn it," Kravis fumed. "I've never been so mad in my life!"

Ted Forstmann had been angry for five years now.

Jim Robinson silently cursed cellular phones.

Slowly, a stream of profanity, like some earthy ticker tape, began scrolling through Forstmann's mind.

Cohen was pacing about, uttering foul things about Kravis.

Boisi stormed out.

Kravis exploded.

Hill bridled.

Strauss was too much of a gentleman to curse Kravis that morning.

Bagley strode around his lawyer's office, waving his arms and violating the dignified hush of Arnold & Porter's Washington office.

Cohen was still fuming.

Forstmann was so mad he felt the blood drain from his face.

Raether was in a foul mood.

Hostility radiated from the man [Kravis] like summer heat from a city street.

Goldstone stormed around the corner into Johnson's office. Spitting mad . . .

He [Kravis] was livid . . . "pissing fire."

Johnson simmered in his office.

For the first time in a month Johnson lost his temper.

Kravis, raising his voice, said, "I'm going to break both your kneecaps!"

"There's a rat fink in the room," Hugel said.

Colleagues remember Maher stomping out of Wasserstein's office from time to time shouting "You asshole!" at the top of his lungs.

Maher exploded.

"This is shit!" Fennebresque ranted behind closed doors.

Maher exploded, kicking the leg of his mahogany desk and slamming his fists violently onto the top.

Ed Horrigan was nearly foaming at the mouth.

Goldstone was on the verge of hysteria.

Horrigan was in a white fury.

As they [Kravis's troops] rode down to the lobby, the elevator was filled with curses and shouts.

Beattie was incensed. "We've been screwed."

"We've been robbed!" Martin yelled. "We've been robbed!"

Shouts of anguish erupted within the Range Rover.

Gordon Rich lost it. He grabbed his gray plastic phone, stretched the cord to its full length and hurled the receiver against the console with all his strength.

"I can make a BMW go faster."

Friedrich Winther
Freight Handler, Dingolfing, W. Germany

By using Federal Express® to fly BMW parts to the U.S. directly from Germany, BMW
dealers can make customers' cars fly out of the shop in just days.

Monday found Johnson in a foul mood.

In no time Horrigan was raging at the board, at Kravis, at everything.

"This is bullshit!" Gutfreund railed.

Roberts hit the roof.

Curses filled the room.

Nusbaum nearly choked.

When Roberts was mad, his lips became small and tight, slits in an angry face.

Roberts was so angry he followed the two members into the bathroom. . . .

Charlie Hugel's gout flared up.

With every bit of anger he [Roberts] tore into Lovejoy.

Horrigan grew bitter and morose.

Henry Kravis, a partner of Kohlberg, Kravis, Roberts, says the X Factor must be instilled in a person—not very helpful advice for a man whose horseshoe rematch with the president was fast approaching.

Fuming, Kravis and Roberts sat back to wait.

"You're [Martin] the most ineffective, immature son of a bitch that ever walked the face of the earth!" Horrigan shouted.

Enough! Somewhere in *Barbarians at the Gate* is this somewhat wistful sentence: "During the '50s, Reynolds was one great, happy family."

I went to see one of these angry men—Henry Kravis himself, who had engineered the $25 billion takeover of the RJR Nabisco company. He agreed to speak with me about the X Factor. The reception room of Kohlberg, Kravis, Roberts (KKR) is on the 42nd floor of the Avon building. The windows look out on Central Park. It was afternoon and the day was extremely clear; I could see north to the Connecticut horizon. I had to squint to see the people below, so that the park itself suddenly seemed like a private enclave. The X Factor, it occurred to me, could very well be engendered by the view from the windows of KKR: it would be hard to sit at a desk, as Henry Kravis does every day, and look out the window and not feel that the world was my oyster . . . that at 11 o'clock, if I wished, I could take the elevator down to the stables and change to ride out to the hounds of the Central Park Hunt. The image of English country-house glamour was enhanced by the muted elegance of the reception room—Stubbs-school paintings of horses hanging on paneled walls, rich carpets on parquet floors. The receptionist sat at a massive desk trimmed in brass with a green leather top. I inspected a painting called *Union Scout*, which showed a group of mounted soldiers emerging from a wood. They are startled, the horses rearing; in the distance the white streak of a lightning bolt is striking a tree. I wondered vaguely if this was symbolic—that the tree was a company involved in a hostile takeover.

Henry Kravis appeared. He was wearing a white collar over a light pink shirt. Slim, elegant, he seemed most collected and not at all like someone from whom anger could rise like summer heat from a city street. We walked through a series of doors that sprung open at the touch of a button—a kind of security procedure. What could they be guarding? I wondered. Surely not the proceeds to finance these enormous deals. Lives, probably. We reached Kravis's office, a smaller and more personalized version of the reception room—family photographs on bookshelves and his desk. We stood at the windows. He pointed out Leona Helmsley's penthouse at the top of the Park Lane Hotel. At the south end is a glassed-in extension that probably contained a large garden shed or small swimming pool—Kravis wasn't sure which. She may be facing jail and a somewhat limited view compared to what she has from the Park Lane Hotel. It was an odd, disquieting sight in that extraordinary view from Kravis's office—perhaps a reminder that things could go very wrong in the world of high monetary usage.

At one end of his office was a sofa and comfortable chairs covered with bright chintz. We sat down. "I've been reading *Barbarians at the Gate*," I said. "Why do all you people in there seem so angry?"

He smiled. "Well," he said, "you'll remember the stakes were very high. People who believe in what they're doing—whether it's writing a book or playing a game—become passionate . . . wrapped up in it. You're in competition. A lot of dumb things were done . . . leaks to the press . . . and certainly that created some of the anger."

I asked if fear, the instilling of it, was a useful ingredient in his line of work.

He shook his head. "Fear of being fired? No, you can't run a company by ranting and raving, because at some point people lose respect for you. Beyond that, because it's a one-man dictatorship, they don't feel they have any role."

I wondered if a kind of X Factor was involved. Was there an overriding principle that guided the workings of KKR?

"Absolutely," Kravis said. "I've always said to the people at the firm that if you don't play your position, then the team doesn't move forward. I don't ever want to hear at KKR 'that's my idea' or 'I did this' or 'I did that.' I want it to be '*we* did this.' We're small enough— we have only 16 professionals—so that George Roberts and I know what everybody's doing. People are 'incentivized' in such a way that they really are pulling for the team, and that's everyone at KKR— from the receptionist at the front door, to the ladies who serve the lunches, to the secretaries, to the senior partners. We are owners in our companies—as opposed to paying everyone a salary, a bonus, and with only two people or so at the top owning all the equity. We think that if the lady at the front desk has an ownership position in every company we buy, she's going to care a little more."

"You mean that secretary out there by the elevator?" I asked incredulously.

"Well, she doesn't put any money in," Kravis said, "but she gets options vested over a period of time. We incentivize her in a different way. We want her to stay here. Down the road we can give her a big check when we sell one of these companies or they go public. But for those in the higher echelons, who *are* involved in a transaction, what's very important is that they put their money where their mouth is—so they have something at risk.

"One of the problems I see in corporations in this country," Kravis continued, "is that managements today are 'renters' of the corporate assets—they're not owners anymore. The day of the Carnegies, the Mellons, the Rockefellers—they're over. What happened was that over the generations the families brought in professional managers; the ownership was dissipated. U.S. Steel was started and built by a family, and then the renters come in with their objective to see how big they can make the company—not how profitable, but how big—and all along living off the assets: the jet airplanes, the golf courses, and so on. The X Factor here with us is that we're owners; we think like owners. When you're an owner you start asking questions that maybe you wouldn't ask otherwise." He shifted in his chair. "Psychologically, it's as though you have a brand-new Mercedes. You polish it; you're not going to want any dents in it, and so forth. Then you make a trip. You go to Avis and rent a nice car. You get a little scratch on the side; you're not very happy about it, but so what. It's not your car. You turn it back in, and you're off to the next thing—there's no real damage to you. So what I call X Factor in business is that you think like an owner."

I asked, "Well, what about the process of *becoming* an owner?"

"Well, of course you have to get there," Kravis agreed. "I've always been a believer in the concept 'don't tell me you can't do it.' I tell my children the word *can't* is not in their vocabulary; just take it out. Some things, of course, you legitimately cannot do, but it's an attitude you should cultivate. I've always had the attitude that I could fall out this window, bounce on my head a couple of times, figuratively, and make myself come up on my feet."

Forty-two floors, I thought.

"I love competition," he was saying. "I thrive on it. I learned it as a young man. I wrestled. When I was in the seventh and eighth grades in Tulsa, Oklahoma, these magazine companies would come around to the school and get the kids out on these magazine drives, contests to see who could sell the most. I just loved that. I'd collect old newspapers in my wagon and stack them in the garage, and then I'd load them up in the trunk of the car. My mother would drive me over to the newspaper recycling plant and I'd get 6 cents a pound, or whatever, for these old newspapers. Each time I tried to do better than I'd done the time before."

I asked, "Well, what was the motivation for this? Was it the money?"

"Oh, no. Not at all," Kravis said. "The competition . . . just not wanting to lose."

"Is it all a game?" I asked. "Was the RJR takeover a contest in that sense?"

"No," he said. "Careers and people's livelihoods were involved. Gamesmanship, perhaps. Letting people believe you're not going to bid. RJR was clearly not a game, because there was too much at stake. But it was a challenge, and I have always liked challenges. People ask, 'Why do you keep working so hard? You've already made a lot of money, you don't need to work.' I say, 'It's pretty simple. It's not the money—clearly not that. If I'm going to compete, then I want to win, and in a moral, ethical framework.'"

"When you talk about a moral, ethical framework, what about the byproducts of buyouts—golden parachutes and such things?"

"I am disturbed by them." Kravis replied. "People are often rewarded for doing a lousy job. The incentive is in the wrong place. It's a 'heads I win, tails you lose' scenario. If I don't do a good job and somebody takes me over, then fine; I've still got my golden parachute and I'm gone. That's wrong. The executive should be on the same side of the table as the shareholders. Unfortunately, that is not often the case. I'm against golden parachutes, except to a certain degree and in certain circumstances. For example, a fellow may have done a very good job for a company, but for some reason the stock is trading at a low price, no fault of management at all, and along comes a raider and throws his people out. In that instance I can understand a golden parachute. What I don't sympathize with is when people have done a mediocre job and walk away with millions of dollars at shareholders' expense."

"Do you think the government should step in?" I asked. "Should golden parachutes be legislated against?"

"Well, the government *has* to a certain extent," Kravis said. "Taxes now make it very difficult to have the same kind of golden parachute one used to have."

He paused and his voice changed slightly, as if he imagined himself speaking to a larger audience. "I wish there was a way to do this," he said. "I'd like to see that the boards of directors of public companies are major owners of these companies . . . and in relation to their net worth. A teacher on the board, or a college president, or a doctor can't afford a lot of stock, but there are a lot of people who *can* afford it. Nor should directors sit on 15 different boards. They should be on perhaps *three* boards and have a real portion of their net worth at risk. I guarantee you in that case they'd hold management accountable.

Right now, no one is holding management accountable. Institutional investors own about 60 to 70 percent of most big company stocks today. If the institution's unhappy, they can call the president, but they'll be lucky to get a return phone call. Or its people will be told, 'If you're not happy, sell your stock.' That's about all that can happen. An institution like the Prudential Insurance Company is not going to start a tender offer takeover fund or a proxy fight to throw the management out. So, until somebody holds them accountable, a lot of managements are not going to change. A big problem is that too many boards work on the principle 'you be on my board, I'll be on your board; we'll be buddies and play golf every week and live across the street from each other, and I won't ask too many questions and you won't ask too many questions on our respective boards, and life will go on.'"

I shifted in my chair and told Kravis that I had always been fascinated by what went through the minds of professional athletes, especially in the moments of stress just before a game. Could he talk about his thought processes as a businessman?

"Well, obviously a lot runs through my mind," he said. "Let's say I'm thinking of buying an RJR Nabisco. I think what could be done with this company, where we could make it more productive, how we could make it grow and make our return on investment more profitable. That's continually going through my mind. We have analysts and consultants come in. Also going on in my mind would be the financing, the right capital structure, how much equity and how much debt should be in place so that the company has flexibility to grow, to move into different areas. Then I think about what happens if the market turns down. I ask myself where the downside is in this investment; how low can the earnings or the cash flow go, given the capital structure? Will the company still be on safe ground? Very important. If I have my downside protected, pretty typically I'll make money all the time. In fact, I worry more about my downside than the upside. At the same time I'm thinking about RJR Nabisco, I'm also concerned with our portfolio companies—more than 35 different companies we've bought since 1976, which we've spent about $68 billion buying. I'm thinking how *they're* doing. Are *they* meeting our expectations? Where can we improve them? What should we do to take the risk out of a particular company by changing the capital structure? I'm also thinking about whether we have the right management in the various companies. I do a lot of thinking very early in the morning. My wife, Carolyne, always kids me because I'll be lying in bed with my hands behind my head. She'll say,

'You're in your thinking position, aren't you?' It's about the only time I do have. During the day I'm lucky to have time to really think, because it's one meeting after another or telephone calls or whatever, group discussions, batting ideas around."

"To get back to the X Factor," I asked, "which in your case seems to have a lot to do with competitiveness. Is that ever a problem?"

"It *is* a danger," Kravis said quickly. "It has to be controlled. Earlier in my life I'd get carried away with a product. For example, I like to fish. The Shakespeare Company was for sale—they make fishing rods. I did everything to figure out how to buy the company, and I could never make the numbers work right. Finally, one of my partners came to me and said, 'Would you just give up on this company? It's not going to work. I'll buy you a new fishing rod and a new reel and you'll be happy.' It was an interesting lesson to me, because you *do* have to look at these things objectively. Mistakes are made a lot of times when one gets too emotionally involved. You can believe in a product, but don't get married to it: things are always changing; you've got to be flexible. All too often people say, 'I've just *got* to own a baseball team. I don't care what I pay for it.' Fortunately, most baseball owners can afford it, so it doesn't make any difference. But God forbid if he *can't*. He's made the wrong decision because he's not being objective. That's what happened to Robert Campeau. Mr. Campeau wanted to be the biggest retailer in the world. His ego got in the way, just *totally* in the way. It wasn't even a matter of being competitive. He wanted to be the biggest retailer; that was the way it was going to be. There was plenty of financing around so he *got* to be the biggest retailer. Look what's happened to him. [Two of] his businesses are bankrupt."

"One would have thought his advisers would have stepped in or at least warned him."

Kravis nodded. "It's very important to have advisers around to bounce ideas off of—to have people you totally trust. I'm not afraid to be told that I'm wrong or that I'm off base. I want smart people around me. The smarter the better. A lot of people make very big mistakes because they have yes men around, because they don't want to be shown up."

"Do you think one is born with your kind of competitiveness?" I asked.

He nodded and said that much of it had to have come from his parents. "My father was in the oil-and-gas business . . . full of risks. He lost all his money in the Depression, got back on his feet, and made a huge success of himself. Independence was the best lesson my parents ever taught me—be on your own. My mother tells me that when I was a little boy she'd come into the room to tie my shoes and help me get dressed, and I'd say, 'No, it's me myself,' meaning 'I'll tie it myself.'"

"Do you think independence can be learned?" I asked.

"I would guess the X Factor is something instilled in you," he replied, "and then it's fostered."

I told him that I was going to play horseshoes with the president. Did he have any suggestions? How would he prepare if he were in my place?

He laughed. "Damned if I know," he said. "I suppose I'd go up to my house in the country, put two stakes in, and throw horseshoes at them. Practice a little bit. That's all I'd do. After all, it's the president's sport."

It was predictable, perhaps, from what he had said about appreciating the downside: it wasn't worth making much of a fuss if you were in a disadvantageous position. Have some fun and get it over with.

He glanced briefly at his watch. "I have dreams every once in a while," he said reflectively. "The dream is that I'm back in school and I can't find my classroom. It's final-exam time. I'm nervous as can be, and I wake up in a cold sweat. Apparently it's a very common anxiety dream for people who set high goals for themselves. It comes out of a combination of anxiety and frustration, because you set these high goals you may not be able to achieve. My father, who's now about 88, still has those dreams."

He looked at me questioningly. "Do you have dreams like that?"

"Yes, many times. But my dreams along that line are a little different. What happens to me," I said, "is that I *find* the classroom where the exam is being given. I sit down, open the blue book, and I haven't got the *slightest* idea what the questions are about. In fact, the thought crosses my mind that I'm in the *wrong* class." I paused. Kravis was grinning. "That's not quite the same as yours, is it?" I said. "I suspect that if you ever found the classroom in your dream you'd sit down, open up the blue book, answer the questions, and get an A."

He smiled and shrugged.

I couldn't resist. "Mr. Kravis," I said. "Are you interested in the takeover, a very friendly one, of a small literary magazine? . . . "

"No," he said cheerfully. "Absolutely not."

"You're looking at one of our biggest priorities."

Dean Martin
Ramp Agent, Newark

At Federal Express, we don't just deliver documents and small packages
throughout the world. We also deliver big packages, big crates, and big containers
throughout the world. In a big hurry.

GETTING
INTO THE
ZONE

When the X Factor really kicks in, the athlete enters a rare and blessed state known as being "in the zone." This is a time-span during which it seems you can do no wrong. And it's not reserved just for athletes; anyone can experience it. Billie Jean King once described it to me: "Oh yes, that's when the ball looks huge and slow as it comes toward you. Those are your good days. On the bad days the ball is quick and looks like an aspirin tablet."

There is no understandable entry to the zone. Athletes speak of it in awe. Lawrence Shainberg, in an article about the zone in *The New York Times Magazine*, mentions Pelé, the great Brazilian soccer player, describing the zone as a near mystical state: " . . . a strange calm . . . it was a type of euphoria; I felt I could run all day without tiring, that I could dribble through any of their team or all of them, that I could almost pass through them physically. I felt I could not be hurt. It was a very strange feeling and one I had not felt before. Perhaps it was merely confidence; but I have felt confident many times without that strange feeling of invincibility."

Shainberg goes on in his article to describe the attempts of an applied sports psychologist named Keith Henschen to train an extra-ordinarily talented 12-year-old archer and Olympic prospect to get herself into the zone. Many of the exercises he gave her seemed directed at "blanking" the mind so that the unconscious would take over the shooting for her. If the conscious mind is involved, the archer worries about the score and will try to make the arrows go into the target instead of *letting* them go in.

Arnold Palmer has talked about this—"in the zone" meaning

having a sense of detachment and being in another world. He compares it to what a musician must feel in the middle of a great performance: not a dreamlike state, but a kind of reverie, in which the focus is not on the present but on the opportunities ahead.

There are two famous remarks relevant to the subject—Yogi Berra's "How can I think and bat at the same time?" and O. J. Simpson's "If you take time to think, you get caught from behind."

I have a Buddhist-scholar friend who is trying to help me learn to empty my mind to facilitate drifting into the zone, which is obviously the state I would like to enjoy for the horseshoe rematch. He has a *zendo*, a meditation place, on his property in Long Island. It was once a stable. There are prayer mats on the floor. He gets me painfully into the lotus position facing a blank wall. He suggests an hour's meditation. As a mental exercise to empty the mind, he recommends that I visualize the faint turbulence left deep in the sea after a submarine has long passed. He leaves me alone. I try. I can hear the hum of bees in the honeysuckle outside the stable window. I try to block everything out. I think of the submarine's wake. It seems to work! I can feel my mind emptying, as if a plug has been pulled out of the bottom of a cistern. But then in my mind's eye a small fish swims by. I watch the flutter of its fins. Then, far beyond the fish, huge in the darkness, I spot the submarine. A port opens and from a cloud of bubbles a torpedo emerges. I can hear the whine of the propeller. I move along in its wake, sleek, like a sea otter. I pause, treading water, and watch it slam up against the side of a freighter. *Boom!* Inside the freighter the captain is in his stateroom shaving. He has an old-fashioned shaving brush. His chin is thickly lathered. He calls out, "Did you hear anything?" The floor tilts slightly under him. A woman appears in the door. She is carrying a small pistol. She asks, "Where's my cat?"

I unwind from the lotus position and stand up. My mind seethes. My legs ache. My friend is facing the wall, meditating. I decide not to tell him about the submarine, the torpedo, and the rest of it. He will accuse me of not trying. I tiptoe out.

The Russians call being in the zone "the white moment." There are other terms for this phenomenon: in Japan, *ki*; in China, *ch'i*; in India, *prana*; in Tibet, *lung-gom*. To pick just one of these, the ultimate stage of *ki* is to achieve an extraordinary unity of mind and body in which athletes, or anyone for that matter (the woman who in a burst of frantic energy lifts a car to get her child out from underneath), can perform feats that astonish everyone, often themselves. The state seems to be beyond what can be achieved with conscious efforts such as mind tricks, willpower, determination, and practice. Sometimes the white moment has astonishing extensions. Examples would be Joe DiMaggio's 56-game hitting streak in 1941; Bob Gibson's pitching performance for the Cardinals in 1968, when his earned run average was 1.12—a record in modern baseball history that, like DiMaggio's, will surely never be surpassed; or, more recently, Orel Hershiser's string of 59 scoreless innings in 1988. All these feats, even to a statistician, surpass the laws of probability to an extent that suggests a level has been reached at which skill is not the only determinant. In other sports, golfer Byron Nelson's string of 11 straight PGA victories in 1945 would compare. In instances closer to the time lapse of a white moment, Wilt Chamberlain's 100 points scored in an NBA game on March 2, 1962, against the New York Knicks in Hershey, Pennsylvania, would certainly apply; so would Los Angeles Rams quarterback Norm Van Brocklin's 554-yard passing game against the New York Yanks on September 28, 1951; Walter Payton's 275-yard rushing game against Minnesota on November 20, 1977; Tom Dempsey's 63-yard field goal on November 8, 1970. I remember Alex Karras, the Detroit defensive tackle, telling me that his teammates were laughing as they saw the New Orleans Saints lining up for this field-goal attempt. The kick is three yards longer than anything made in the 20 years since.

That is the point about these records: they seem almost unassailable. Chamberlain, for example, broke his own record of 78 when he had his 100-point game; the best performance by another player is David Thompson's 73 points against the Detroit Pistons on April 9, 1978.

Perhaps the most striking example of this phenomenon at work would be Bob Beamon's amazing 29-foot-2½-inch long jump during the Mexico Olympics in 1968. In an event in which advances are made in quarter inches and very rarely, Beamon jumped more than a foot over the previous mark—"jumping into the next century," as a felicitous phrase in *Sports Illustrated* described it. For a number of years, no other long-jumper placed in the range of 28 to 29 feet; Beamon's entry looked like a printer's error in the record books.

What is odd is that Beamon—because he had achieved the unconscious state one looks for in *ki, ch'i, prana,* whichever—was not really aware of what he had done. I interviewed him some time later. I asked him if perhaps he had a mental catalyst, a spur to help him jump so far, if he imagined something snapping at his heels, a pack of wolves? He shook his head. No. Nothing like that. His mind was blank. He told me that he had hopped out of the sawdust of the jumping pit knowing

A true case of being "in the zone": Bob Beamon jumped more than a foot farther in the 1968 Mexico Olympics than anyone on record ever had.

that he had made a good jump, but nothing about the jump struck him as extraordinary. He looked across the infield grass at the scoreboard, where the distances were measured in meters rather than inches, and began to transpose the figures to see how he had done. The roar of the crowd startled him. He looked around to see what they were cheering—perhaps a pole vault somewhere in the arena—and realized that the stands close to the track were emptying and that a crowd was coming for *him*, arms outstretched, eyes shining with excitement. Abruptly, he was aloft on their shoulders, being borne around the arena in triumph. It was frightening, he told me, because the reason for all this was not clearly set in his mind. He kept calling down from the shoulders of his supporters to find out exactly what he had done.

Being in the zone is a phenomenon one can experience in other professions—especially those in which bursts of creative energy occur. One would guess that "absent-minded" scientists and theorists spend a lot of time in it. Archimedes was stepping not only into a bath but into the zone when he figured out that an object submerged in water displaces its own volume, and was so pleased with himself that he ran into the street naked, shouting "Eureka! Eureka!" He was almost surely in the zone when he was run through by a Roman soldier after the Battle of Syracuse, oblivious to everything that was happening around him and working on a mathematical figure in the sand.

The literary world is full of examples of creative-energy surges that seem to have little or no connection with the conscious mind. One reads that Robert Louis Stevenson's plots were provided for him in his dreams by what he called his "Brownies." Hervey Allen, the author of the big, steamy bestseller *Anthony Adverse*, spoke of an angel-like creature that danced along his pen when he wrote—a kind of metaphysical recorder. Jean Cocteau said in an interview, "I feel myself inhabited by a force or being—very little known to me. It gives the orders; I follow." E. L. Doctorow speaks of the last stages of writing a book as giving him the "exhilaration of a free ride—like a downhill ski run."

Ernest Hemingway, in an interview I did with him, described a day in Madrid when the bullfights were snowed out and he found himself—though this wasn't the way he put it—in the zone. "First I wrote 'The Killers,' which I'd tried to write before and failed. Then after lunch I got in bed to keep warm and wrote 'Today Is Friday.' I had so much juice I thought maybe I was going crazy, and I had about six other stories to write. So I got dressed and walked to Fornos, the old bullfighters' cafe, and drank coffee, and then came back and wrote 'Ten Indians.' This made me very sad, and I drank some brandy and went to sleep. I'd forgotten to eat, and one of the waiters brought me up some bacalao and a small steak and fried potatoes and a bottle of Valdepeñas.

"The woman who ran the pension was always worried that I did not eat enough, and she had sent the waiter. I remember sitting up in bed and eating, drinking the Valdepeñas. The waiter said he would bring up another bottle. He said the señora wanted to know if I was going to write all night. I said no, I thought I would lay off for a while. 'Why don't you try to write one more?' the waiter asked. 'I'm only supposed to write one,' I said. 'Nonsense,' he said. 'You could write six.' 'I'll try tomorrow,' I said. 'Try it tonight,' he said. 'What do you think the old woman sent the food up for?'

"'I'm tired,' I told him. 'Nonsense,' he said (the word was not *nonsense*). 'You tired after three miserable little stories? Translate me one.'

"'Leave me alone,' I said. 'How am I going to write if you don't leave me alone?' So I sat up in bed and drank the Valdepeñas and thought what a hell of a writer I was if the first story was as good as I'd hoped."

To help me perhaps sneak into the zone, a friend of mine has sent a catalog of inspirational tapes. The face of Dr. Paul Tuthill is on the cover—young, with a Freud-like beard and a pleasant, confident smile. In the catalog he quotes Thoreau: "Each of us has a Genius within us, waiting to be released." This is done, the catalog would have me believe, through subliminal messages—the subconscious hears the messages, which are synchronized and hidden within the music. The sports available do not include horseshoes, though boxing, skiing, bowling, weight-lifting, and racquetball are listed. So I picked bowling since the arm motion is similar. I also ordered "Self-confidence" and "Defeating Discouragement." The musical selections included bluegrass, country, reggae, classical. I picked "Inspirational Flute," which the catalog informs me combined flute sounds with "the natural rhythms of a babbling brook" to lift one above "the humdrum thoughts of everyday."

The catalog says what the subliminal messages would be if the sounds of the flute with its babbling brook rhythms were scraped away. Letters of certification attest that these messages are indeed there. They struck me, frankly, as somewhat peremptory and unimaginative. The stop-smoking tape apparently intones incessantly

"Smoking stinks!" You'd think Dr. Tuthill might have enlisted Gregory Peck to recite the Surgeon General's warning. The tape entitled "Stop Math Anxiety" has as one of its subliminal messages "Math is easy!"

The catalog makes the tapes, though, sound extremely potent. Indeed, there is a warning about using two of them ("Maximum Strength" and "Stop Smoking") at the same time. "Each is a difficult challenge and should be addressed individually."

The tapes I ordered have arrived, and I play them on occasion. My friend asked me if I thought they were helpful. I said I didn't know. "A lot of flute music," I said. "It's hard to tell whether I have been lifted above the humdrum thoughts of everyday."

"What's that?"

"Never mind," I said. "I guess we'll find out in the Rose Garden."

Also for inspiration, I have turned to an old friend, Peter Buterakos, a cemetery-plot salesman from Flint, Michigan. Somewhat resembling a barrel-chested elf, he is famous throughout the Midwest for his inspirational speeches and especially his wild bursts of cajolery. I heard him give a speech on business administration before 4,500 in Flint that went on for more than an hour. He punctuated what he was saying by tossing various props out at us, including live pigs ("there are pigs in the business world!"); rubber daggers, blood-red at the tips ("at the top, people are waiting to stab you in the back!"); and rubber snakes ("competition can turn good men into snakes!"). He finished off his talk by plunging through a mock brick wall wearing a Superman outfit to demonstrate that "anything can be overcome."

Despite his small stature, he calls himself, and just about everyone else as well, "Big Man." The phone rings. "Big Man?" His voice is so high and imperious that the receiver must be moved back from the ear.

"Er—yes?"

"Big Man! It's the Big Man."

I had met him not long after I had been with the Detroit Lions. He had come to training camp to give an inspirational talk, during which he had set off a cherry bomb ("life is full of abrupt changes"). It had rolled behind him and blown a big chunk of plaster out of the wall. Joe Schmidt, then the Lions coach, liked to say that Buterakos kept his audiences not only on the edge of their seats but usually two or three feet above them.

I telephoned him.

"Big Man," I said. "I'm going down to play horseshoes with the president."

The news didn't surprise him at all. "Why not, Big Man!" he shouted.

"I need a boost," I said. "I need some ideas."

"You need to throw him off balance," Buterakos said. "Blow his mind. Get him kind of uneasy, so he's even nervous picking up a horseshoe. Right?"

"Yes," I said. "But remember that the Secret Service is standing around."

"Well," Buterakos said, "I'd start off by calling him Lefty."

"Lefty?"

"He's left-handed, isn't he? If he isn't, it's even better. Blow his mind. Then what you do when you're warming up is to pick up a

Peter Buterakos, a cemetery-plot salesman in Flint, Michigan, had some unique advice: he told the author to take a horse to the rematch, topple the animal, and wrench its shoes off in front of the president.

"Try telling your kid you fly a warehouse for a living."

Mark McNair
Pilot, Indianapolis

By using Federal Express planes to deliver everything from computer parts to airline tickets just when they're needed, companies are discovering that they can keep inventory costs from soaring.

horseshoe and lob it through a window of the White House. Then you turn and apologize. You say, 'Lefty, I hardly know my own strength today. I'm all pumped up. I've got the strength of Samson.'"

"Well . . . "

"Hey, get this, Big Man! When you arrive at the White House you're wearing all the uniforms from the teams you've played with. Wear your Detroit Lions football helmet. You shake hands with the president. Then you take off the helmet and under that you're wearing a New York Yankees cap. You raced cars, didn't you?"

"Well . . . "

"You're wearing an asbestos suit, bright red. You climb out of that and you're wearing your Boston Celtics T-shirt with your name on the back. You should wear a pair of skates out to the horseshoes."

"A pair . . . "

"You played for the Bruins, right? It'll blow Bush's mind. He'll ask, 'What are you wearing those things for?' You tell him, 'Lefty, I just got these skates *sharpened*. I can stop on a *dime*.'"

I tried to interrupt. "Hey, Big Man . . . "

"Listen to this, Big Man! You bring two people to the White House with you. Guess who."

"Who?"

"Mike Tyson." He paused for emphasis. "And the Hulk."

"They may have to carry me in," I ventured. "What with those skates and all. I have very weak ankles."

"Why not?" he shouted. "They lift you up under the elbows—Tyson and the Hulk—and they carry you out to the horseshoes like you're a kind of valuable weapon!

"Then what you do is bring a high school band with you, not a good one, Big Man, but one that's only been practicing for about a week. They know maybe two or three tunes—'Pop Goes the Weasel' and 'The Star-Spangled Banner.' Blow his mind! The music sheets always fall off those little stands, right? And get *this*, Big Man!"

"What?"

"You bring your own horseshoes," he shouted over the phone. "You say, 'Lefty, I don't trust your White House shoes. I've brought my own!' Tyson and the Hulk start pulling on a rope and from around a bush comes the biggest goddamn horse you ever saw in your life—a Percheron type of animal. It comes clomping in wearing the shoes you'll be using. It'll blow the president's mind!"

"How do I get them off?" I asked innocently.

"Hell, Big Man, you get the Hulk to topple that horse right over and you *wrench* them off. You tell the president, 'Nossir, nobody, I mean *nobody*, is goin' to tamper with my shoes.'"

I told him I was wanted on the other phone. "Thank you, Big Man," I said. "I'll be turning all this over in my mind."

He was still chattering away when I hung up.

The president has been playing golf at Kennebunkport. The papers are full of it. His game is unique—speed being an important consideration. In fact, the score seems less important to him than the time it takes to get around the course; the local pro refers to a Bush round of golf as "cart polo."

I read that the president has found some new motivational phrases to go along with his game. One of them is "Mr. Smooth." "All right, now, Mr. Smooth," he murmurs to himself as he stands over the ball. Another is a name—Vic Damone, the crooner of the postwar years. When the president has sunk a long putt or wins a hole, he cries out "Vic"—short for victory—and adds on "Damone."

Golf has traditionally been not only the politician's game (Eisenhower, Kennedy, Ford, Tip O'Neill, Quayle, et al.) but also the CEO's favorite outdoor pastime. It provides a kind of microcosm of corporate life without any of the complexities—challenges (the course), options and decisions (which club), financial involvement ($5 Nassaus), competition (playing partners), success (the sinking of a long putt), and failure (the duck hook)—all of this played out in a spirit of camaraderie over a summer day in an environment rich with the accouterments of success: beautifully groomed and landscaped fairways and greens; the country club with its oak-lined taproom; the locker room with its carpet soft to the feet on the way to the shower; a shoe-shine attendant whose first name is known to everyone and his last to nobody. Best of all, the institution is totally permanent. One can play in it far beyond retirement years; there is a handicap system that puts one, whatever age, on par with the immortals.

The CEO's real-life ultimate in golf (besides being asked to play hurry-up golf at Kennebunkport) is to be invited to play in the AT&T Pebble Beach National Pro-Am Tournament. Not only do the CEOs enjoy the privilege of hobnobbing with the more powerful of their kind, along with screen and sports stars, but they have the chance to appear on national television with the pros as their partners. There can hardly be a CEO in the country who does not recall James D. Robinson III, the CEO of American Express, known familiarly as "Jimmy Three-Sticks" from those Roman numerals, calmly chipping a shot over a trap and into the hole of the 18th at Del Monte—on national television, what's more. This was probably CEOism at its most glorious, with hardly an executive in the country not leaning out of his armchair to catch it: "Look at ol' Three-Sticks, that son of a *bitch!*"—half in envy, half in admiration.

Recently, I called up Robinson to talk about it. I got through to him largely, I think, because I told his secretary I wanted to ask him about "the shot."

"Tom Kite was my partner," Robinson said. "We came up to the 18th—the final group, huge crowd circling the green, national television—and I found that I was looking at a delicate chip shot over a sand trap. *Well,* I thought, *there's a good chance I'll knock the ball into the trap, or worse, skull it over the green and hit someone in the crowd. It'll be the end of me.* I thought about picking up. Tom was about to win the tournament, but we weren't going to win the team event. Instead, I turned to my caddy and I said, 'Let me have the sand wedge, because I'm going to sink it.' And I did!"

"Like a dream," I commented. "You were in the zone."

"To this day it's the single most important thing I've done in my life."

I blinked and asked if perhaps being the chairman of American Express wasn't comparable.

"Oh, no," Robinson said. "Clearly, by the acclaim I get traveling around the world, I can tell. People come up and they say, 'I saw that shot!' They don't say, 'I recall the day you became chairman.' That year I went up to Albany with the New York City Partnership [a business lobbying group], which we do every year, to meet with the Senate leadership. Before that shot I always had to stand in line and introduce myself. This time, Warren Anderson, the majority leader, came right over to me, with David Rockefeller and a lot of others waiting, and he said, 'That was the most impressive shot I have ever seen!' He then proceeded at some length to tell me about a shot *he'd* made while playing with Bob Hope. From then on we were bosom buddies.

"There's a whole practical side to sports," Robinson went on. "In a sports environment you get to know something about people, how they come across, how they manage their emotions. . . . "

I asked, "Would you have trouble promoting someone who . . . well, suddenly snapped a putter across his knee after missing a shot?"

Robinson demurred and said he didn't take people out on the golf course to promote or fire them. "Periodically I'll take some of our management down to the Augusta National or out to Cypress Point," he said, "because those are legendary courses. So (a) they really appreciate it, and (b) it gets us off for a couple of days so we can get to know one another in an environment other than behind a desk or in the conference room. They do the same sort of thing with *their* customers. It's an appropriate part of a total process."

I asked what his golf handicap was. An eight. Physical fitness is a big thing with him. Every morning he does from 600 to 1,000 sit-ups. He has all the machines. American Express has a physical-fitness program called Wellness.

"Good Lord," I said. "How long does it take to do 600 to 1,000 sit-ups?"

"Twenty minutes to a half-hour. It sets an example. It's important to have a fit and determined work force."

He got talking about conducting management affairs, that they should be handled in the manner of a "benevolent Lombardi" (a nice oxymoron) and that the focus should be to create a team that would, as he puts it, "win Super Bowls every day, not simply annually."

When he gets talking about his company, he talks this way, I was told afterward—little snippets from speeches exhorting his troops: "The will to win is part of the fiber of this country." "A determination to win is vital in the business context." "You've got to have a core set of values . . . march to the quality drumbeat." "I have often said," he told me, "that I want on my tombstone the word *quality*."

"I beg your pardon?"

"Quality. That's the one thing since 1975 that I've focused on most at American Express."

Theologian and author Michael Novak offered several insights concerning the Pope, baseball, and chopsticks.

Afterward, I wondered about 'quality' on one's tombstone. Someone wandering through the cemetery, not knowing it was a company catchword, might assume Robinson wished to have it descriptive of *himself*, which, while doubtless true, might seem . . . well, a bit cocky. Some other less self-serving possibilities came to mind. Why not something to commemorate his great shot at Del Monte on the 18th? "The Chipper," with his dates underneath. Or at the very least, if the American Express association was to be identified, why not the famous slogan "Don't leave home without it"? Or surely more intriguing: "I left home without it."

"Does the Pope play golf?"

I was on the phone with Michael Novak, a distinguished theologian whose book *The Joy of Sports* is perhaps the best on the impact of sport on society. Novak is a passionate fan. His spirits are lifted after a bad day simply by the knowledge that on television that night he'll be able to watch the Dodgers in Montreal.

At one point he had written, "I have never met a person who

disliked sports, or who absented himself or herself entirely from them, who did not seem to me deficient in humanity . . . such persons seem to me a danger to civilization."

I had reached Novak to ask him about this. He agreed that perhaps he had put it a bit strongly. "I do feel, though," he said, "a firm spiritual ground with people who have been involved with sport. Unless you've gone through that particular kind of struggle involved in sport . . . there's a certain lack. Sports teaches you how difficult things are."

That was when I asked about the Pope and golf. "Does the Pope . . . I mean, what sort of background does the Pope have in sports?"

"He's an excellent skier."

"Oh?"

"He was a soccer goalie. I don't know about golf."

The thought of the Pope sailing down a mountain with his clerical robes billowing out behind settled for an instant in my mind.

Novak was saying that he had been rereading Tocqueville, about the way Americans approached commerce, contrasting it with the Europeans. The main difference is that Americans approach everything with the zeal of the revolutionary; they delight in chance and risk . . . a pervasive element all across America.

"Sports—baseball first—celebrates this, and very powerfully."

"Why baseball?" I asked.

Novak laughed and said that baseball had powers even he hadn't suspected. He had asked a Korean businessman to explain the economic recovery and development of a country broken by war.

"What the Korean said was that they had studied the Japanese very carefully and discovered two secrets. In order to develop, a country needs either chopsticks or calligraphy, preferably both, *and* to play baseball. I had laughed, and the Korean had said, 'No, no, I'm serious. Look at China. They use chopsticks, but they don't play baseball. Look at Cuba. They play baseball, but they don't use chopsticks.'

"And then he explained. Chopsticks teach a fine coordination between the brain and the hand—crucial, since the finest quality in manufacturing is going to win in the marketplace. Secondly, Asians have always been collectivists—the Confucian idea of family, community, ancestor worship, and all that—and the result is that they have no theory of the individual. He said that baseball teaches them that. Baseball singles you out. The lone player approaches the plate. The ball moves toward a single player who must deal with it."

Novak went on to say that baseball offers the best characterizations of John Locke, of the Constitution. "The framers were trying to build an association in which the individual would play a larger role than ever before. Baseball is a magnificent celebration of that."

"So individualism is the key?"

"Well, it doesn't quite work out that way in the real world. We have evolved more toward football," Novak replied. "The first thing you have to do starting a business is hire a lawyer. Second, you have to work with suppliers. Customers. Teamwork! That's probably more appropriate. I tried to explain this once to a cardinal at the Vatican, where everyone thinks that American business is all rugged individualism. I asked the cardinal to try to imagine what it must be like to be president of a huge company like General Electric, with almost a hundred affiliates, each with its own manager. There are only four or five hotels in the country with sufficient accommodations for all these managers (and their wives) to meet. I asked the cardinal to try to imagine what it's like for a CEO to take someone's word over the telephone when he sees him only four times a year, yet on whom he must count . . . and the degree of trust and camaraderie that has to be developed. It's not quite like a football team; it's never that intimate. But if you don't have the essence of teamwork, things will start to go bad—and quick. Still, football is close to the image of corporate life. Committee, committee, committee—just like huddles. Working things out. Strategy sessions. Progress is slow, careful. The love of surprise, ambush, initiative, enterprise—Tocqueville saw all of this as unique elements of the American character long before the invention of the game."

I wondered if sports as a metaphor wasn't often too simple.

"Oh, life is much more complicated," Novak said. "Sports doesn't offer any guidance in how to get along with women. Our sports were really developed for men, so they pretty much exclude half the human race. Sports by no means teaches you everything, but it is the best field for teaching fundamental ethics. For example, one lesson that's so crucial in sports is that you learn about losing. Learning how to accept a loss is a supreme test—not the winning but the losing."

Novak told me about a German professor, Eugene Rosenstock-Huessy, who was teaching ethics at Harvard and found that his references to European history, its great figures, did not make the same impression on students that they had in his home country. He slowly discovered that for every key point he wanted to make he could find a parallel in the sports Americans played.

"He began studying baseball, football, and so on," Novak said, "and found that he could go far by teaching the basic insights of ethics through lessons learned in playing sports—discipline, excellence, failure, spirit, suffering, seizing the moment. He found that play constituted not an interlude for Americans but a foundation of their intellectual and cultural lives."

thought it would be interesting to talk to Billie Jean King about the X Factor. I had once played her in an exhibition in the New York Coliseum. The court was makeshift—a carpet laid down and mesh netting to keep the balls from flying out into the display area among the sporting-goods exhibits. It was all over very quickly. Since the match was an exhibition, and presumably to entertain the crowd grouped behind the netting, I assumed King would keep the ball in play. Not at all. She bore in behind a big serve. My desperation lobs banged against the ceiling.

She had no particular need to call upon an X Factor that day. We became friends; she was certainly someone to check with about winning characteristics.

First, I asked her about Novak's comment that sports in America, especially team sports, had neglected women.

She agreed, though she felt that schools and colleges were doing something to alleviate the problem. "The team sports *are* more important," she said. "Individual sports like golf or tennis teach you to be on your own—courage, independence, endurance, dealing with pressure. But the team sports teach 'people skills,' management know-how. They provide a training ground for so much," she said. "Cooperation, communication, working toward an objective. Body and mind working as one."

"What's the best part of it?" I asked.

"I love the challenge, the opportunity to do my best at a critical moment. I think that's the way champions feel," she said. "When the opponent is serving, a lot of people say, 'Please, God, make it a double-fault.' But for me, I *want* it. Don't you?"

I winced and admitted that I was in the less confident school. "No, I pray the other guy's serve is going into the net. Indeed, I try to will the ball into the net." I told her that I spent so much kinetic energy trying to will a double-fault that I had very little left over to deal with the ball when it came over the net.

King grinned and said, "Yes, Charlie Brown. Well, that's not to say that champions never think like that. But generally they say, 'Give me the ball. I want the opportunity.' That's the X Factor at work. Champions relish the moment. It's *f-u-u-u-n-n*"—drawing out the word as if to relish it—"when it's close. I used to dream about

GETTING INTO THE ZONE

moments like that when I was very young, and I think how lucky I have been to be able to actually experience them."

Had she ever purposefully eased up in a match so she could get to that pressure point that gave her so much pleasure?

"I've been accused of that," King said, laughing. "I hope not, though subconsciously that may be so. The subconscious is so strong."

I told her about my horseshoe match with the president and that I would be playing him again. Did she have any suggestions? How would she prepare mentally?

"I read a lot of psychology books. I get buzzwords from them."

I asked for an example.

"'Exaggerating' is one," she said. "If a match gets close, I slow down my rituals. If I bounce the ball twice before serving, I'll bounce it slowly, or repeat the ritual, bouncing it four times, *exaggerating*. I make absolutely sure that I have total clarity, acuteness, focus. I try to visualize (another buzzword) where I'm going to hit my serve. That's what President Bush was probably doing when he said 'remember Iowa'—visualizing a ringer, the horseshoe going through the air on a certain trajectory and landing around the stake. It's all an exercise in total commitment—technical and visual. I go through all this before I start. Then I feel the adrenaline flowing, and I know the moment has come: *Go!* and I commit myself. You're totally involved in the moment. That's what good concentration is."

I said that with all these things going on in her mind, it was hard to imagine that she could toss up the ball.

"No, no," she said. "All of this is before the commitment. Too much thinking and you're going to jam the computer."

I laughed and said I was reminded of Tim McCarver's remark. The former catcher and now baseball commentator had said about similar circumstances that "the mind is a great thing as long as you don't have to use it."

"That's it." She wished me luck in the horseshoe match. "Get yourself some nice buzzwords," she said.

"あなたの街をとても良く知っている
フェデラル・エクスプレスです。"

Jun Funabashi
Courier, Tokyo

"When it comes to the international shipping business,
we know our way around like the natives. Because we *are* the natives."

THE REMATCH

I wrote a letter to the president saying that with spring weather coming my thoughts were increasingly turning to horseshoes and the prospect of a rematch. I didn't tell him about Dr. Tuthill's inspirational tapes or Peter Buterakos's big horse. Nor did I say that I had not touched a horseshoe since we had last played at the Naval Observatory. I did mention the X Factor and that I hoped we would have a chance to chat about it, even if briefly. I said I was ready to leave New York at a moment's notice. I added that I had purchased a cowboy hat.

Within days a letter arrived from the White House. The president wrote that he was so looking forward to the match that he was "already suited up in his National Horseshoe Pitchers Association jacket." The question was where to play and when. "The all-weather clay," he informed me, "better than the Georgia red clay [à la Observatory] that I know you favor, is ready now. Five to 10 degrees more in temperature and it would hold any shoe you fling. . . . Here we could do it almost any day—after work, or skip lunch and tee it up. At Camp David we have a classic setup as well. . . . How about a biathlon: shoes and tennis doubles?"

We decided on Camp David. He said for me to bring anyone I liked, and I took my son, Taylor, who is 13. He was nervous about it. He found it hard to accept that he was facing a weekend with the president. "I don't know about this," he said.

"You can cheer me on at the horseshoes," I told him. Taylor's voice is breaking, often cracking in midword, so that with an exhortation such as "Come on, Dad!" the first word is a boy's soprano, clear as a bell, and the *Dad* deep, a kind of bassoon note. I wondered if this might throw off the president. Taylor is a good athlete, especially at tennis; he is the junior champion where he plays in the summer. "I'm sure you'll be involved," I said.

We left on a Saturday morning shuttle for Washington. I forgot my cowboy hat. Tall-crowned with a blossom of feathers in the front, it made me feel less a cowboy than a Las Vegas crapshooter.

"Damn!"

My son looked over.

"I forgot my hat."

He looked startled, which was not surprising since he has never known me to wear a hat.

"It was a cowboy model," I explained. "A good-luck hat. I've never worn it except to try it on, but I feel lost without it. My X Factor hat!"

It was raining heavily when we landed. At Camp David, pale-green guest cottages are spread throughout the woods, each with a golf cart and bright baby-blue bicycles out in front for the occupants. The cottages are named after trees: Red Oak, Aspen, Laurel.

No sooner had we put our bags down than a quick knock sounded. We looked up expecting a functionary to help or advise in some way. The president was standing in the doorway wearing a tall cowboy hat. I stared at it. He ducked his head as he came in. I introduced him to Taylor. "You're going to have a great time," the president assured him in a loud, cheerful voice. "Lunch in half an hour. No ties. No coats. After lunch we start the sports."

He addressed all this to Taylor, as if the afternoon was a kind of conspiracy between them. "Yes, sir," Taylor said, looking up, his eyes shining with excitement.

Before lunch the president gave us a tour of his working quarters. There was not much to see: a conference room, with its long mahogany table decorated with models of the presidential planes and helicopters down its length, and a pint-sized office barely able to contain more than four people at a time.

The president showed us a large framed map of the U.S.S.R. he had received from Gorbachev, which showed a kind of nooselike arrangement of symbols representing U.S. military bases encircling the Soviet Union—less a gift, perhaps, than a reminder of how threatened the Soviets feel. I asked how accurate the map was. "Very," the president replied.

In the center of the room, leaving even less space to get around in, was a glass case, which served as a coffee table. It enclosed a display of a small covey of quail crouched amid the autumn leaves around a stump, beautifully mounted and reflecting, of course, the president's love of quail-shooting. The president told us that Mrs. Bush—because of her love for animalkind—did not think much of the quail group, and that was why it had been relegated to the president's office.

"Here, Taylor. Let me show you something else Mrs. Bush doesn't approve of," the president said. In a small hallway just off his office he showed us a large framed cardboard cutout of a man's head and torso—the silhouette target used on pistol and rifle ranges. In the center of the torso were scrawled the names of Bush and Marc Cisneros—the latter a top American general in Panama. Cisneros had discovered it in Noriega's headquarters during the Panama operation and thought the president would like it. The cutout was bullet-ridden—20-odd holes, mostly in the head, fired from a 9mm pistol about 15 feet or so away, presumably by Noriega. Cisneros had hand-written a description of the circumstances along one side of the cutout, ending with the salutation "Merry Christmas!"

"Wow!" Taylor said.

Also on the wall was a wicked-looking military knife removed from one of Noriega's "dignity" battalions, and next to it the original mug shot of Noriega snapped in the Miami jail. A true trophy wall!

"Wow," Taylor said again as we walked into the living room.

"Dad?" he whispered to me.

"Yes?"

"The quail table . . ."

He wanted to know if I thought the quail had anything to do with *Dan* Quayle. In his classes at school Taylor is beginning to be taught Freud, associations, symbols, and so forth.

"You mean symbolically the president is keeping Dan Quayle under wraps, under glass in his office?"

"Something like that."

I grinned and said I doubted it.

By chance, I caught sight of Quayle's face on a television set murmuring in the corner of the living room.

"Look, sir," I said to the president. "It's your vice-president."

"Yes," the president said without turning his head. "He's back from South America."

He didn't seem at all interested. It struck me how divorced he seemed from all the complexities of his office. The desk in his office was bare except for a coffee-cup warmer. On the rare occasions when there was a phone message, it was a family matter. More and more, I had the feeling that Taylor and I were enjoying a weekend stay with a country squire who didn't have anything on his mind except perhaps how his prize springer spaniels were going to do in the local dog show. His weekends were completely for relaxation.

Lunch was announced. The entire house party had gathered—the president and his wife; his brother Jonathan Bush, his wife, Jody, and their two sons, John Jr., who is at Wesleyan University, and Billy, who is a star lacrosse player and captain of his team at St. George's School; his daughter-in-law Margaret and her two children, Marshall, age 4, and Walker, age 4 months. The only outsider besides Taylor and me was Lloyd Hatcher, a friend of Margaret Bush and a recent graduate of North Carolina, who was working on the White House staff. Young Walker Bush was passed around the room, as one might pass a salver of mints, to be inspected by family members. Dogs were underfoot—Millie, an English springer spaniel named after a Texas friend, Mildred Kerr. Millie succeeds a cocker spaniel named C. Fred, who was deaf toward the end of a long life and would snap at anything not coming from the front. Millie's son Ranger was also on the premises. Both were constantly on the move, their claws skittering on the bare floors between the rugs. Millie carried a tennis ball between her teeth so that it seemed a natural extension of her face. The president took it from her and lobbed it across the room.

"Uh-oh."

He had hit Mrs. Bush, who was on the telephone with someone, on the side of the head.

Mrs. Bush hardly took notice. "George," she said into the phone, "just hit me on the side of the head with a tennis ball."

"Serious business," the president said.

We went in to lunch and started talking about buzzwords. I mentioned *Vic Damone*, for victory. Barbara Bush laughed. She said that when the information about Vic Damone became public, got into the papers, they had met the Damones. (He is married to Diahann Carroll.) Vic had thanked President Bush for the publicity; he was "getting started on a second career."

During lunch the president continued to make Taylor feel at home. Among other things, they talked about preparatory schools. The president mentioned that his attachment to Andover was far stronger than to Yale.

"Why is that, sir?" I asked.

The president shook his head ruefully. "Well, Yale burned me in effigy some years back. That tends to linger on."

The afternoon sports program (it was still raining heavily) started with bowling—a caravan of golf carts, black umbrellas raised, riding along the paths to a low-slung building, again pale green and hard to spot amid the trees. The president skipped the bowling (for a nap, we were told), but he joined us in midafternoon for the game called "wallyball," which is volleyball played on a racquetball court. The president, who was wearing gray sweatpants and a T-shirt that read UNIVERSITY OF WASHINGTON SERVICE, lined up on the opposite side of the net with Taylor, Lloyd

Hatcher, and a presidential aide named Tim, who was possessed of a hard off-sidewall serve that caused great confusion in the ranks of the opposition—namely myself, Jonathan Bush, and his two sons.

The noise within the confines of the court was deafening. As soon as the ball was in the air the uproar began—yells of encouragement, yelps of appreciation at good retrieves, each point ending with shouts of delight on one side of the net and moans of despair, apologies, and recrimination on the other. Our team—none of us had played wallyball before—was getting the worst of it. Across the net Taylor was playing with great spirit. His favorite athlete is Boris Becker; like him he tends to sprawl headlong after shots, skidding on the floor. The president beamed down at him. "Hey, Taylor!" he called out. Their team won six games. After each game the president called out, "How 'bout another?"

We played for more than two hours. Billy, one of Jonathan Bush's boys, went out with a sprained shoulder. That didn't stop the fray. A mammoth Marine, or perhaps a Secret Service man, was hurried into action on our team. Eager to please, he sprang around the court. We won a game. "How 'bout another?" the president asked.

Finally he said, "Well, maybe that's enough." Handshakes, and then the president led us to the exercise room just off the racquetball court—Nautilus equipment, stationary bicycles, treadmills, rowing machines. Some of them were being used by military personnel—husky men with crew cuts who wore slightly embarrassed looks when the president walked in, as if they couldn't decide whether to spring off the machines to attention or to continue pumping away. The president nodded and spoke to some of them. He programmed a bicycle machine for Taylor. He tried one himself. When I left to get ready for dinner he was lying on his back, encompassed by an apparatus that was supposed to strengthen his lateral arm movement. He's thinking about the horseshoe match, it occurred to me.

Sunday morning the president and I got a chance to talk about the X Factor. I sat opposite him in his little office, my cup on the quail (or Quayle, as my son thought of it) coffee table. When I mentioned the X Factor, the president immediately said that he knew what I was talking about. In his case he felt the X Factor had something to do with his reaction to crowds.

"Crowds, sir?"

He went on to say that 30 or 40 years ago crowds had sometimes affected him adversely. He described playing in what he called "one of those deadly pro-ams" on a golf course near New Orleans.

"I was playing with Mike Souchak," he remembered. "I was playing to an 11 handicap, which is pretty good. I remember the crowds getting bigger as we got near the 18th. I then shanked three shots in a row. Watching was a taxicab driver who must have left his cab on the street to come out to the golf course; he was still wearing his badge number—3280 or whatever—up on his cap. He'd seen me shank the first one, giggling behind his hand. When I shanked the second, and I stepped up to hit the third shot, which was about a half nine-iron, I heard him say (I've got rabbit ears) to the guy next to him, 'You really want to see somethin', watch *this* cat.' And I shanked it again! A lot of guffawing!

"Well, that was the situation then. In those days I found I did better one on one, *mano a mano*. With people watching, the pressure made me knuckle under. When I was about 12 or 13, playing in a country-club tournament, I ordered my aunt out of her seat at court-side because she was making too much noise."

"I can't imagine that you got away with it," I said.

"Of course not," the president said. "I had to write a long letter of apology. But that was all a long time ago. Since I got into politics and thus more comfortable with the roar of the crowd, it's been a 180-degree turn."

"You look forward to the pressures?"

"That's right. Rising to the occasion. Maturity has a lot to do with it, of course. When the horseshoe pit was inaugurated at the White House, with quite a crowd there, I was asked to throw a couple of shoes. It went through my mind, *well, suppose I step up and don't even get it in the clay*. I went ahead, and darned if I didn't get a couple of ringers." He grinned. "I quit immediately. Timing is very important."

"So the X Factor has a lot to do with what you gain from experience?"

"Learning how to fight back. They say you're 17 points down in the polls. So I'm going to show 'em. Fight back. I find that as the pressure mounts, the adrenaline flows, and it pushes you to be better. There's a relationship. Of course, you can have the adrenaline flowing and screw it up.

"It all goes back to what your mother taught you: do your best, try your hardest. It's funny, but here I am, the president of the United States, and that advice from my mother, who is highly competitive and loves sports, still affects almost everything I do— try your hardest, and if you know you're doing that, criticism rolls off like water off a duck's back. That would not have happened, incidentally, before the X Factor started working *for* me instead of against me. I got over it when I matured, got into the big leagues of politics."

I wondered how it was possible to face that barrage of comment every morning, the columns, the cartoons . . .

"You can't afford to bristle and get tense about it," the president said. "The parallel in sport is some guy yelling at you from the stands, or the coach in the locker room. You can't take it personally. You just determine, well, we'll show 'em."

"Do you think of politics as a kind of game?" I asked. "It has so many of the same metaphors."

"Campaigns, yes. But not so much in the day-to-day politics. If you're in a fight to sustain a veto or convince Congress to compromise on Clean Air, there's competitiveness involved and a certain determination to try to win. With something like Panama there's obviously that same tension and anxiety, and then after the operation a great sense of relief . . . but I'm not sure how I'd compare that to sports or a game. It's too serious. Lives are at stake. The emotions from sport are different. I'm not in that league in sport where my livelihood depends on it. So sports are a relaxation for me, the competition, the camaraderie. Playing horseshoes with my sons is as much fun as anything I do in life. Pure relaxation."

"A lot of people say that an important element in sports is learning how to lose," I said.

"I'm a traditionalist. There is something about holding your hand out to the victor that is proper, and I'm not necessarily talking about white-flannel etiquette. It's certainly so in politics. The guy who walks off the field whipped and is a poor loser lives with that and sometimes in counterproductive ways . . . people remember: you were such a bad sport in the primaries that you cost the victor the final election because of the way you behaved. So there's a clear analogy to sports."

"What about business?" I asked.

"I've been out of it for so long," the president said.

"The leveraged buyouts, the takeovers . . . "

"Much of it is offensive to me," he said. "The rich do this just to get richer. It's become a game to some degree, but it's not particularly pretty or attractive. Maybe I've been in government too long, but I see some of the golden parachutes, the golden handshakes—thank you very much, a gold watch, and $30 million—and then I compare this to public servants, who dedicate their lives to government, and I think there's a disconnect here."

The two Bush boys rode past the office window on their blue

bicycles. They dropped in, the dogs at their heels.

"Down, Ranger!" the president said.

"Do you think regulation might be a solution?" I asked.

The president leaned back. "They're free to do it, and I'm not going to propose legislation to do anything about it because I believe in the freest possible market. But that doesn't mean I can adjust either to enormous debt or the magnitude of personal compensation that goes on these days."

"You can't just make it a question of conscience."

"Conscience is such a subjective quality," he replied. "Two honest people can differ on how something should be done. Fundamentals should be the guiding principle—doing the right things, upholding the values shaped by family. That's why I worry so about the dissolution of the family, the disadvantage that a kid starts off with if he or she doesn't enjoy a normal family life, a mother to read to him, and so forth."

"How does sport enter into this?" I asked.

"I don't think sport can be overemphasized. Fitness, of course. But it keeps telling you to go back to fundamentals—keep your head down, left arm straight, keep your eyes open, swing when you shoot, don't move your head . . . hundreds of basic rules. And on a less practical but highly important level, sports gives us its heroes— people who in some instances dispense that X Factor we've been talking about. I gauge people in sport not so much by performance but by sportsmanship. I tell people that my favorite sports hero is Lou Gehrig. He stayed in there; he was good (batted above .300 for years), and he played every game; he provided a certain sense of strength and stability and leadership to the team. I gather he was a very decent man, and when he left there wasn't a dry eye in Yankee Stadium because of the respect for his character as well as his ability."

The president looked at his watch and said it was just about time for the church service. Then it would be on to the day's sports activities.

These started with skeet shooting. The range was manned by Marines in camouflage gear. The president had been given a new shotgun, a 20-gauge Weatherby. He was very proud of it. He showed us the silver inlay work on the breech—a beautiful design of quail, the bird he especially likes to go after. Just above the safety was an inlay of a horseshoe stake ringed by a horseshoe. "They thought of everything I like," he said. "But then look at this." He brought the gun up so I could read what was

"It's 3 a.m.
Do you know where your package is? I do."

Dennis Connelly
Trace Agent, Boston

No matter what time of day or night you need to know about your packages,
documents, or freight—no matter where on earth they may be—our tracking networks
allow our Customer Service Agents to track them down for you. In seconds.

inscribed in barely visible letters on the barrel. MADE IN JAPAN. He shook his head. "The rest of it, the stock and so forth, was all made here," he said defensively.

He was pleased with his shooting. He had become adept at it during the war, shooting clay pigeons off the stern of his aircraft carrier. Twice as good as the rest of us—his brother Jonathan, his two nephews, and me—he led us quickly from one shooting station to the next, almost as if there were an internal rhythm that had to be applied. His targets disintegrated in fine black puffs of residual dust. We moved too slowly for him, fumbling with safety catches, dropping shells, ignoble on the doubles, and watching the pigeons float quietly to the grass untouched.

Next, tennis. We drove up to the courts in our carts. The president was wearing a San Francisco Giants baseball cap and a Washington Senators sweatshirt, presumably given to him by an entrepreneurial type, hoping baseball would return to the capital. I suggested that the president play with my son, since I knew Taylor would want to tell his grandchildren one day that he had partnered with the president. My partner was Lloyd Hatcher, who was slim and fast and had played briefly on the Virginia Slims circuit. The level of play was high and exciting. Taylor tumbled to the court à la Becker and made spectacular retrieves. The president was agile, especially at net, and they combined well as a team. The president kept up a spirited chatter. A badly missed shot involved "a high humiliation factor." An over-zealous angle was referred to as the result of "a high arrogance factor." Once I heard him call out after he had hit a strong shot between us, "Hey, threading the needle . . . the X Factor!"

They were ahead in the first set 5-3, but we caught up and won in the tie-breaker. "How about another?"

It was chilly. A wind sighed through the pines. Beyond the fences, three Secret Service men with backs to the play stood looking out into the woods to check on anything moving out there. They could have been taken for birdwatchers, bored with tennis, and on the watch for a red-eyed vireo fluttering in the undergrowth. Beside them were valise-like bags that contained, I was told, Uzi automatic weapons. A phone at court-side suddenly rang.

The president was serving; his second ball was in the air. He was obviously startled—the familiar indoor sound of a telephone so odd to hear emerging from amid the trees. His serve went out by a foot. He strode across the court to pick up the receiver. We watched him, wondering what sort of news was so demanding as to interrupt his tennis game this weekend. He bent over as if to hear better and then straightened up. He looked over at me. "It's for you!" he called out. He held out the receiver.

Oh, my God, I thought as I hurried toward him. *It's Buterakos, the Big Man! He's at the Camp David gate with a high school band and the Percheron! He's demanding entrance.*

Thankfully, it was not the Big Man, but a friend trying to get a message to me about a dinner party that night in New York; to his astonishment, he had been put through to the tennis courts. He recognized the president's voice. "My God," he said to a friend with him. "I think I've just been speaking to the president of the United States."

We played better in the second set. Perhaps the phone call had a slight psychological effect. Lloyd Hatcher got her game going—possibly because she didn't like the idea of being beaten by a 13-year-old, even if his partner was the president of the United States.

The president and I left by golf cart for the horseshoe court, leaving a contingent playing tennis. I told the president I had forgotten my cowboy hat. He grinned and said that he wouldn't bother going back to the house to fetch his; we'd play even.

The horseshoe facility is very fancy. It has a board with round pegs that are moved along a bar to keep track of the score. At both ends a bucket of water hangs from a crossbar, with a towel alongside to wipe off the shoes. The pits at either end are filled with the puttylike all-weather substance the president had described in his letter. The horseshoe slaps into it with the sound of a wet towel being dropped on the tiles of a bathroom floor. Rather than burrowing into soft surfaces such as sawdust or Georgia clay, a shoe that lands on its side tends to be rejected as if the surface were made of rubber; it leaps wildly out of the pit. I discovered this to my dismay during our warm-up tosses.

A Secret Service man took up his position by the scoring board to move the pegs. The match began. Across the macadam path, 4-year-old Marshall moved among the paraphernalia of a little playground. Her mother was with her. Occasionally Marshall called across to her grandfather. I was reminded of Jenna at the match at the Naval Observatory.

The first game did not go well at all. We were playing to 21 points rather than to 15 as we had the first time. The president jumped out to a 7-0 lead. I landed a ringer on one of his, which doubled my score to 6 points. This was the last time I scored in that game. The man from the

Secret Service moved the president's peg inexorably along the board. My peg remained permanently stuck at 6, as if fixed by glue. The president played very quickly, much as he had on the skeet range. Almost as soon as the last horseshoe of the set lofted toward the opposite stake, he was striding down the court. I had no time to step into the woods, press the palms of my hands against my temples and commune to get myself into a better frame of mind, to latch on to some of the principles I'd been hearing about that were part of the X Factor. Every other shoe I threw seemed to land vertically on an edge rather than horizontally. On more than one occasion the shoe struck the wooden border of the pit with a harsh clang and set off down the macadam walkway like a hoop hit with a stick.

The president won the second game 21-1. As we played, through my mind flitted a number of images and impressions—a mishmash of what had been suggested over the months by my advisers: focus, concentration, confidence, even snippets of athletic catch phrases not at all pertinent to horseshoes ("keep your eye on the ball," "never up, never in"). A curious background humming in my ears may well have been Dr. Tuthill's babbling brook.

Across the macadam path Marshall called out from her swing. "Hey, look how high!"

"Very high," the president said, looking over and smiling appreciatively.

The third game began. The man from the Secret Service started moving the president's peg. His granddaughter hopped off her swing and came over to have her coat unbuttoned. The president bent over and slipped a thong off a wooden button. He straightened and threw three ringers in a row. "Hey!" he called out.

"I see you've changed your pitching style, sir," I said. "Throwing the shoe laterally rather than how you did it the last time we played." This professional appraisal must have seemed utterly presumptuous coming from someone who had scored only 1 point in the last 10 minutes.

"A little power outage there," the president said politely as one of my horseshoes bounced in front of the pit.

I remembered Billie Jean King's advice, one of her buzzwords— exaggerate, slow everything down—so I dawdled. I tried to block everything from my mind. My Zen friend's submarine appeared. I could sense the president's impatience as he stood alongside. I threw the horseshoe. It hit on its edge and bounded angrily toward the scorekeeper, who stepped aside to get out of its way.

The president took his turn. "Nice shot," I said. "Lovely."

My peg had not moved on the board. Billie Jean King appeared in my mind's eye again. Her mouth opened. She was going to say something. Nothing emerged. A high school band played in the distance. A nagging voice, perhaps that of an angry stage director, began to take over. It is familiar. It has manifested itself in most of my participatory stints. "Idiot!" it called. "You're making a *fool* of yourself."

The president's last shot was a perfect ringer. I had not scored a point since the middle of the second game. A debacle! I avoided the eyes of the gentleman from the Secret Service who had been moving our pegs, or more accurately, the president's. I hoped the president wasn't going to cry out "Vic Damone!" He didn't.

We got in the cart and headed up for lunch. "Not my day," I said. I wondered what the president was going to say to make me feel better about what had happened.

"I won't say anything at lunch about the horseshoes," he said with a big smile, "if you don't mention what happened at tennis."

It wasn't over. Just before lunch Jonathan Bush suggested a quick game of tiddlywinks. The president agreed instantly—with no sense that he was being asked to indulge in a game that could hardly be called . . . well, *presidential*. He oversaw setting everything up. The table had to be the right height. The stewards hastened through the room. A blanket was produced and spread over the table. Various glasses and cups into which to chip the little disks, or winks, were brought in by the stewards and discarded as being too tall or too shallow. "John, do they play this game in the Philippines?" he asked. A steward shook his head. "A shame," the president said. "My mother is the great champion of the family."

The president picked me as his partner, perhaps reckoning that yet another loss at his hands might be too much for me, that I would crack under the humiliation and ride off into the forest on one of the blue bicycles. Taylor was partnered with Jonathan Bush.

We lost. The president stared at the table. "A rematch!" he called out. "Have to have a rematch."

"We'll hold up lunch," Mrs. Bush said to the head steward. This was said with no suggestion of impatience or resignation, but simply in the sense that something far more important had come up than sitting down to a luncheon table.

In the second game the president and I surged into the lead, but then we faltered. I chipped a disk far over the cup, off the table and into his lap. "It's a knack," the president said as he put the disk back. "My mother could run off a string of six, seven. Just automatic from anywhere on the table."

The outcome of this game was the same as it had been in the first. We lost when Jonathan Bush chipped three disks into the cup.

"Not my day," I said to the president. "I let you down."

On the flight back to New York, I asked Taylor what he would remember most about his weekend with the president.

He thought for a while. "I'll remember him hitting Mrs. Bush in the head with the tennis ball." He laughed. "I'll remember how he came and knocked on the door of our guest house and came in that first time with his cowboy hat, and how he made us feel at home. After that he never seemed like the president but just a very nice person, about the nicest person I ever met. Then just before he got on the helicopter to go back to Washington, I looked and he was wearing a brown suit and a red tie, and he was the president again. Just amazing!" He paused for a moment and then he said, "It was the best time I ever had in my life."

I wondered vaguely if he had been turned from an Independent into a Republican.

"What about you, Dad?" he asked.

"My bones ache," I told him. "I've never gone through anything quite like that. I'll remember the stewards rushing around trying to find the proper-sized cup for tiddlywinks and a blanket for the table. I'll remember how badly I played at horseshoes and how well you played as the president's partner."

"I served a double-fault when we were ahead 5-3 in the first set. The pressure . . . "

"Doesn't compare to my collapse at horseshoes," I assured him. "One point in two games."

"Did you talk about the X Factor?" he asked.

"For a while," I said. "For him it seemed a lively combination of things—sportsmanship, confidence, concentration, fundamentals, adrenaline, maturity, trying your best always . . . and perhaps the most interesting thing he said was that in his case he had learned to perform better *because* of the public gaze rather than in spite of it."

I told Taylor that I had been reminded of what had been said about the prizefighter Muhammad Ali: that he needed the roar of the crowd to sustain him, much as Anteus needed to touch the ground to support his strength; a journeyman fighter could beat Ali if they fought in a telephone booth.

"I should have come down to watch you play horseshoes," Taylor said. "It might have helped."

I sighed and said it wouldn't have made any difference if he'd brought down the entire population of Maryland.

"He had his X Factor working for him," I said. "Mine didn't seem to be anywhere in sight."

After a moment he asked, "What does 'effigy' mean?"

"Well, it's a kind of dummy people make," I said, "usually of straw and old clothes, of someone they don't like. Then they hang it from a tree with a rope around its neck or burn it. It's a rather excessive way of letting off steam."

Taylor was looking out the window.

"You're thinking of the president's remark about Yale?"

"Yes," he said. "I guess they didn't get to know him, those people." He was still looking out the window. I could see the skyline of New York beyond.

I was glad he'd come. He'd exemplified a bit of the X Factor himself—flying around the tennis court, winning with the president at wallyball, and beating him at tiddlywinks: a far better record than mine.

As for me, a curious axiom of John Madden's came to mind. I had heard the former Oakland Raiders coach and now television commentator pronounce it at some point. It was: "Don't worry about the horse being blind. Load up the wagon." Madden added that he never had known quite what it meant, but it *sounded* pretty good. I think I have the gist of it, though. It seems appropriate enough. . . .

"We didn't just start an air express service. We started a revolution."

At Federal Express, we do a lot more than deliver packages and freight swiftly and dependably to more than 120 countries worldwide. We work in partnership with companies to design and operate the most sophisticated business logistics systems in the world. This allows companies to expand their markets, improve productivity, and compete more efficiently in a rapidly-changing global economy. You could call it revolutionary.

Additional Copies

To order additional copies of *The X Factor*
for friends or colleagues, please write to
The Larger Agenda Series, Whittle Direct Books,
505 Market St., Knoxville, Tenn. 37902.
Please include the recipient's name, mailing
address, and, where applicable, title, company
name, and type of business.

For a single copy, please enclose a check for $11.95
payable to The Larger Agenda Series. When
ordering 10 or more books, enclose $9.95 for
each; for orders of 50 or more books, enclose
$7.95 for each. If you wish to place an order by
phone, call 800-284-1956.

Also available, at the same prices, are copies
of the previous books in The Larger Agenda Series:
The Trouble With Money by William Greider,
Adhocracy: The Power to Change
by Robert H. Waterman Jr.,
Life After Television by George Gilder, and
The Book Wars by James Atlas.

Please allow two weeks for delivery.
Tennessee residents must add 7¾ percent sales tax.